While I Walk

Solo Adventuring in the Vast, Beautiful World

Rachel Durchslag

FOSS & FLORA

ISBN: 979-8-9871257-0-0 (paperback); 979-8-9871257-1-7 (eBook)

This book is a nonfiction memoir. No events have been altered and no persons fabricated. However, in some cases, names and other identifying information have been altered to protect the privacy of the individuals involved. The stories in this book have been told as truthfully as possible while recalling experiences glazed with nostalgia, peppered with pain, and embellished with gratitude.

The advice given herein may not be suitable for every person or every situation. This work is sold with the understanding that neither the author nor the publisher are held responsible for any results accrued from the information in this book.

First Edition

Cover design: Amy Froelich
Illustrations: Caroline Smith
Page design: Maggie Powell
Editors: Kris McCoy and Beth Beasley

For more information, please visit: www.whileiwalk.com or email: rachel@whileiwalk.com

Of all the paths you take in life,
make sure a few of them are dirt.

—UNKNOWN

Advanced Praise for *While I Walk*

"Your favorite hiking book has just arrived. With fourteen spectacular hikes, plus a goldmine of tips and tools, *While I Walk* is your sherpa and your muse, essential reading before you buy your ticket and pack your backpack. Rachel Durchslag offers a generous balance of detailed information and inspiring insights, opening a window to the interior journey of solo hiking. This precious gem will change the way you think about our earth and the possibility of experiencing her beauty more deeply."

—Mary Davis, author of *Every Day Spirit: A Daybook of Wisdom, Joy and Peace*

"Filled with empowering, insightful nuggets from her hikes across the globe, *While I Walk* fuels the imagination for your first—or next—hiking adventure. Whether meditating while walking alone through ancient Japanese forests, or overcoming personal doubts and physical challenges slogging up trails in Nepal, Rachel reminds us of the connections between nature and self, which bring us joy, freedom, and the ability to shift perspective. By the time I'd finished the first few chapters, I had my boots laced up and was planning my next trip."

—Amy Field, author of *Sola: One Woman's Journey Alone Across South America*

"In *While I Walk: Solo Adventuring in the Vast, Beautiful World,* Rachel Durchslag reminds us of the power of place and the extraordinary things we can learn from the world, and about ourselves, when we travel to both iconic and lesser-known regions. Durchslag is a seeker, and there is one constant that makes this book far more than a travel guide. Each external journey the writer embarks on is accompanied by an internal, deeply spiritual quest. She reminds us that beautiful, remote spaces—and the daunting journeys that often must be undertaken to get to them—can reveal to us not only who we are in the wild, but what we can become in our day-to-day lives."

—Anne K. Ream, author of *Lived Through This*

"The exquisite way in which Rachel writes about her external adventures will inspire you to pack your bags and put your hiking boots on and get out on the trail to explore the wild places for yourself."

—Rajyo Allen, author of *Fumbling Towards Freedom*

"Rachel Durchslag is a world hiking adventurer. Her descriptions show her passion for the various trails, and her writing comes from the heart. This book is for hikers, travelers, adventurers, and dreamers."

—Danny Bernstein, author of *DuPont Forest: A History*

"*While I Walk* captures the poetry of the planet with its beauty, grandeur, and many offerings of the unexpected. Rachel's narrative carries us to unexpected moments of delight, awe, and yes, courage when the going is unexpectedly challenging. She weaves the poetry of the planet together with the poetry of her inner journey of transformation."

—Gary Whited, author of *Having Listened*

"Refreshing, inspiring, and educational, in *While I Walk* Rachel bares her heart with touching and honest vulnerability. This unique memoir also serves as an informative guidebook to duplicate Rachel's bucket list adventures. I will revisit this book often when I'm contemplating where I should walk next!"

—Nancy East, author of *Chasing the Smokies Moon*

"From Nepal to Alaska, Tasmania to Ireland and beyond, Rachel shares a journey of self-discovery with personal insights, practical tips, and delicious recipes. A must-read for those who feel the call of the trail."

—J.F. Penn, author of *Pilgrimage: Lessons Learned from Solo Walking Three Ancient Ways*

"This book is a soul-awakening journey into the outdoor enthusiast's heart! Not only did I feel like I was traveling the world going through these incredible, breathtaking hikes, but Rachel also shares her inner joy, her challenges, and the obstacles she had to overcome to follow her dreams. It is truly inspiring, as well as packed with practical and helpful advice, recipes, and guidance for the avid hiker! Highly recommended!"

—Dr. Shannon South, author of *Grow Your Business By Growing You*

Contents

Preface

*Those who contemplate the beauty of the earth find
reserves of strength that will endure as long as life lasts.*

—RACHEL CARSON

A tattoo adorns my left wrist. The curved series of small black dots does not follow a particular pattern but instead marks the beginning of a trail. Just as I continue to explore mountains throughout the world, the number of dots on my wrist increases as both a tribute to, and a map of, the places I have been and the lessons I have learned while walking.

The birth of my tattoo tradition came to me the day after I finished the Camino de Santiago pilgrimage in 2016. That final day of walking had brought me to the shores of Muxía in Spain, where I spent the last hours of daylight sitting at the ocean's edge watching the region's famously wild waves reach improbable heights. My fellow pilgrims sat scattered among the craggy rocks, and I felt a sense of deep reverence for our combined journeys mingling with the ocean air. Although I'd expected this final evening to be filled with joyous laughter and congratulatory banter, the night was relatively quiet, save for the sounds of one solitary flute. Its music embodied both the sweet and the melancholy, perhaps reflecting the feelings in our collective hearts.

I did not want my journey to end.

My Camino was not a linear one, as you'll learn in the first chapter of this book. I'd started my first major solo hike with all the wrong intentions. I wanted to be one of the fastest to complete the 500-mile trail, proving my hiking prowess. I also wanted my kamikaze hiking pace to make it impossible for anyone to keep up with me. My greatest Camino fear wasn't the long hours or arduous climbs but instead having to confront my extreme social awkwardness. I strategized that if I started early, walked quickly, and took only necessary breaks, none of the other hikers would be able to keep up with me—freeing me from the trap of labored chitchat. So I hiked far too fast, and for that I paid dearly. Ten days into my trip, a stress fracture left me unable to walk. My Camino was over.

I returned home to North Carolina feeling physically broken and emotionally defeated, having not achieved my dream that had burned so brightly and for so long. It had taken so much hard work to make my Camino happen: hours of intense training in the mountains, figuring out how to take a month off from my life, and seemingly endless evenings poring over packing lists and countless books about the journey. I was beyond devastated that I did not make it in the end. If I had just slowed down, listened to my body, and embraced humility, perhaps I would have been able to complete my journey. Instead, I was forced to limp back into my life to try to put the pieces back together.

Eventually, the fog of self-blame lifted, and the resolution to do my next Camino differently took root. I began the challenging process of healing both my fractured leg and broken heart. A knee-high walking boot forced me to slow down, and I began to take stock of what had happened. I used my time in therapy to investigate my internalized need to push myself too hard and override the cues of my body. I analyzed my fear around interacting with strangers. And I spent time journaling and getting my head in a better space so that when my leg had healed enough to walk again, I would be ready not just on a physical level but on a spiritual one as well.

Four months later, I once again found myself on the Camino—with just the slightest whisper of pain from my leg fracture to remind me of my previous attempt. As a sign of my dedication to do my trek differently this time, I went so far as to write a contract—with myself. I agreed to stop every two hours to take a break, whether I was tired or not. If I felt lonely, I would ask nearby pilgrims if they wanted to walk with me. And in recognition of all that my body was doing for me, I would send it love and appreciation every step along the way.

Not surprisingly, my second journey on the Camino was radically different than that first failed attempt. I deepened my mindfulness practice and learned to relish taking in the details of my surroundings. I drank leisurely Americanos in small cafes in medieval towns and even invited strangers to join me at my table. And most importantly, I sought connection with others. Though I will always be a solo hiker, the Camino taught me the value of making friends along the trail, and those friendships are among my most treasured today.

Reaching Santiago de Compostela at the end of my journey was nothing short of electrifying. Seeing the cathedral's spires outlined against the blue Spanish sky felt like a homecoming. And celebrating with my Camino family over lemon beer and tapas in the town square felt like a tribute not just to our walking journey but also to the person I had become thanks to my pilgrimage.

Instead of ending my journey in Santiago de Compostela, I decided to push on to the coast of Spain, where in ancient times people believed the sun fell off the edge of a flat earth every night only to be resurrected in the east the next morning. At the conclusion of that three-day journey, I found myself on the edge of a cliff in Finisterre on what happened to be the Jewish New Year, the holiest day in my tradition. As the sun made its final descent beneath the ocean's expanse, I felt a profound sense of completion.

My walk was over. I had reached Muxía, watched her roiling waves create a barrier between land and sea, kissed a cute German pilgrim, and fell asleep with the crashing of the Atlantic for a lullaby. In the morning, I boarded a bus back to Santiago de Compostela feeling disoriented and sad. Something inside me had been ignited on the trail, and I'd felt more alive while walking than perhaps ever before. Leaving the Camino felt like I was leaving a part of my heart behind.

And so, on the day before my departure from Spain, while waiting for my dad to meet me in Santiago de Compostela to celebrate my grand accomplishment, I once again set out on the Camino's path to be with the trail one final time. I wandered through gardens and old waterways until I reached the hilltop, with views of the

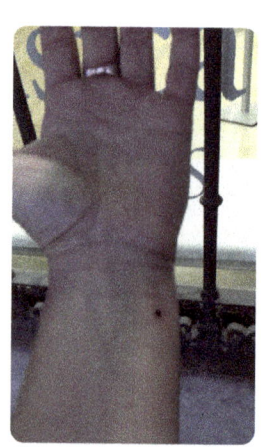

Cathedral of Saint James in the distance. My tears flowed freely as I thanked the Camino for all she had given me, for the opportunity to return to her trails, and for the person I'd become throughout this experience. And then, almost as if in response to my prayer, I heard an unmistakable message: "You need to remember that in your life you are always walking your Camino. No matter where you are, no matter what the journey, you will forever be a pilgrim in this world."

Then I had a vision of getting a dot tattooed on my wrist so that I would never forget this truth.

I found the local tattoo shop and, with the help of an interpreter, asked for a solitary dot to be tattooed on the inside of my left wrist. I instinctively knew where the dot had to go without understanding exactly why. But after I'd returned to the United States and asked an acupuncturist friend about this particular location, she told me that in Chinese medicine it represented spiritual growth in the heart.

Since my first Camino, I have continued to be a walker across the world, traversing the trails of some of the most magnificent landscapes imaginable. I have pushed myself past physical limitations, shed my fair share of tears when I didn't think I could go any farther, and learned things about life—and myself—that would have been unavailable to me any other way. I've eaten mouthwatering meals in mountain huts, survived on cans of chickpeas

when vegan food was impossible to find, and imbibed glasses of wine with fellow walkers from all around the world. I've experienced rainstorms, injuries, lost luggage, broken gear, and countless other practical challenges. And I have seen sunsets that left me breathless, glacial seas that brought me to tears, mountain vistas that opened my heart, and wonders that forever changed me. Each trail has taught me a specific, significant lesson, and these lessons are the dots that continue to multiply on my wrist. They serve as a reminder of the pilgrim I continue to become in this world.

This book emerged from a time when walking the world was no longer possible. After the pandemic hit in March 2020, I had to find new ways to feel that sense of awe and earth connection without boarding planes and discovering distant paths. And though I deeply longed for the mindfulness and joy I always experience in the mountains of foreign lands, this pause was an invitation to fall in love with the mountains of my home in the southeastern Appalachians. These mountains have taught me that I do not always need to go far away to find an expanded version of myself. As long as I can still walk, listen, and wander along a mountain trail, I am still honoring the Camino inside me.

Introduction

There were dark days during the pandemic when even brushing my teeth seemed like a daunting task. Feeling the claustrophobia of being caged in my house day in and day out, I often stared into the abyss of depression and felt dangerously close to falling in. I did my best to cope and find *some* joy. I binged-watched Netflix. I categorized my recipes. I cleaned out my closet over and over. But nothing brought my normally sunny self back to the forefront. My husband and I came up with a term to capture how we were living: malaising.

So when a few friends recommended that I spend my time in quarantine writing a book about travel, I laughed. I scarcely had enough energy for household tasks and uncomplicated distractions. In all honesty, I was barely changing into clean yoga pants every day, let alone feeling productive enough to do something new. The early days of COVID were about surviving, not creating.

But the message kept coming: "You should write about your travels," my friends insisted.

And my answer continued to be no.

But then, for my forty-third birthday, I received a gift that changed my perspective. It was the book *Women Who Hike* by Heather Balogh Rochfort, an excellent exploration of inspirational women hikers in the United States. And though I enjoyed reading about the lives of these hiking pioneers, I especially appreciated how each chapter ended with logistical information for completing that woman's favorite hike.

As I made my way through the women's profiles, I thought, what if I could write a book that would allow me to share my experiences in an inspiring way? What if my writing could be a catalyst for other women to feel safe putting on their hiking shoes and embarking on solo adventures throughout the world?

Once I conceptualized my book not as a telling but as an invitation, the words came easily. And now that it is complete, I hope that reading about some of my adventures (and misadventures) will inspire you to board a plane to places like France, Jordan, Chile, and Nepal to begin your own journeys of expansion. Almost every trip in this book can be done solo or with a group, so if you decide that hiking solo is not your thing, don't despair! In most of these places, there will be fabulous fellow hikers there excited to create incredible trail memories with you. But if you *are* open to going solo,

I hope this book shows you how possible and transformative it can be to travel alone. More information on solo travel can be found in the FAQ section.

Now to the structure of the book. Each chapter focuses on a different hike I have completed, starting with statistics about that particular trail. This information is followed by an artistic map drawn by my friend Caroline Smith. These maps are a tribute to my dot tattoo and help the reader see at a glance certain trail information, such as elevation, distance, and whether or not a trail ends where it begins. The points radiating out represent significant camps, peaks, or rest stops along the trail. The elevation is listed in meters on the left side. Distance between each landmark is listed in kilometers on the stem leading to the dot. If the name of the first dot on the left side is the same as the dot on the right side, the trail is a loop.

At the end of each chapter, you will find logistical information about how to complete that particular hike. I also highlight a few words in the regional language and share a handful of meaningful photos I captured along the way. And then I offer a recipe from that region. Let me explain why.

I am a vegan who loves food. Eating dishes in other countries is one of my favorite ways to connect with where I am. And eating local food after a long day on trail makes each bite that much more delicious since I've worked hard for my hunger. People often assume that eating vegan while hiking is difficult, and sometimes it is. But I have found restaurants and hotels throughout the world to be beautifully accommodating. Likewise, I've been profoundly touched by kind and generous hosts and their willingness to meet my dietary restrictions. I include a vegan regional recipe for each hike so you can sample what deliciousness might await you at the end of a hard day or climb. Even if veganism is not your thing, these recipes are still bursting with local flavor.

And at the end of the book, there are FAQs and helpful lists and tips to provide guidance on planning your own hiking and outdoor journeys. Thank you for taking the time to explore with me. Happy trails—adventure awaits!

Camino de Santiago, Frances Route

May and September 2016

DIFFICULTY: Moderate | LENGTH: **491 miles (790 km)** | ELEVATION GAIN: **15,044 feet (4,585 m)** | DURATION: **30–35 days**

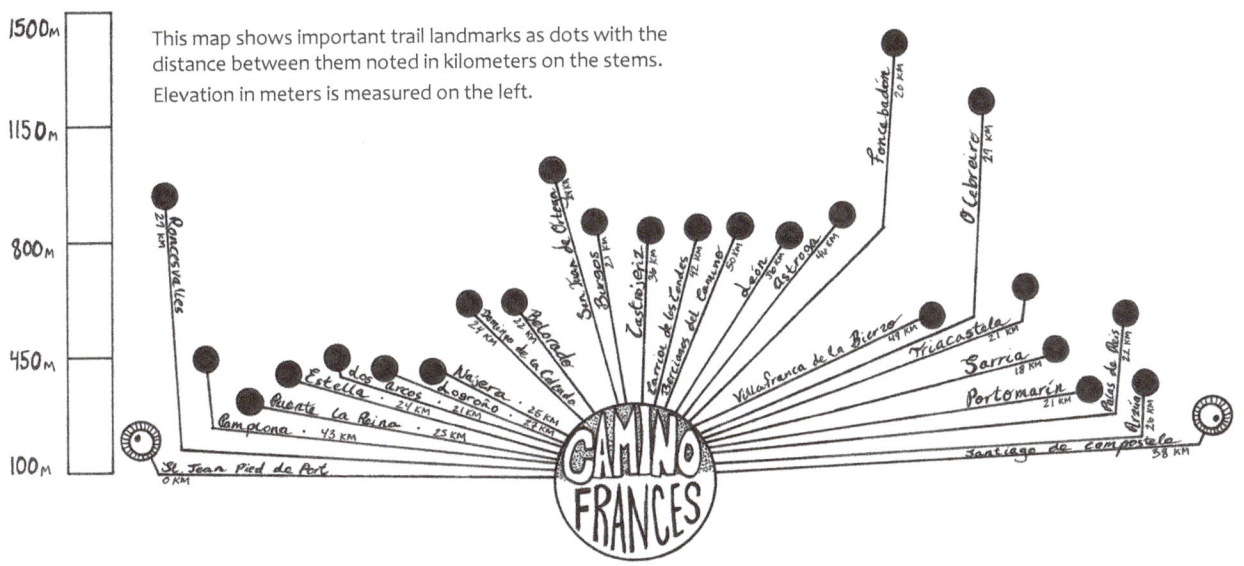

This map shows important trail landmarks as dots with the distance between them noted in kilometers on the stems. Elevation in meters is measured on the left.

A walk in nature walks the soul back home.

—MARY DAVIS

●∘●● LESSON... You are always on a pilgrimage. ●●∘●

This is where it begins. The whisper of an idea. A far-off contemplation. An invitation to the new way I will be in the world.

The Camino de Santiago is a melody that summons many to her, from the pilgrims of medieval times to the contemporary soul seekers of the modern era. This pilgrimage through Spain holds deep sacred space for those willing to meet her there.

I came to the Camino because I love hiking, travel, and all things spiritual, but never before had the three come together in a singular profound experience. Choosing to walk the Frances route felt like an honoring of what already nourished me, yet with the added challenge to take it to the next level. Could I really live for an entire month with only what I could fit in a small backpack? Could I overcome my stifling shyness to create friendships with other pilgrims from around the world? Could I walk for miles each day and find contentment in the rhythm of my steps and the pace of my breath? Could I share communal living spaces with strangers and forgo my accustomed comforts for the opportunity of growth?

I was eager to find out.

I had traveled alone for a significant amount of time only once before. It was the previous August when I decided to board a plane to Iceland and drive solo around the island's famed Ring Road. I wanted to see what it would feel like to be completely alone for ten days. To embrace solitude in a way I never had before. To have full control of my itinerary and live every day as an open adventure. Though I figured Iceland's otherworldly, lava-formed landscape would be unparalleled in its beauty, I anticipated that I would most likely struggle during my time there—facing loneliness, boredom, and even embarrassment at being alone while others were traveling with their partners or friends.

Surprisingly, I loved every minute of it.

I relished the feeling of waking up and knowing I could welcome in whatever adventure I chose that day. Without the distraction of conversation, I was able to tune in to the subtle sounds of the land. Its oceanic melodies. Its stunning silence. Its crackling glaciers and rushing rivers. As I drove over bumpy roads, dodging herds of sheep that seemed to materialize from the fog, I sang loudly and off-key in my car. I ate simple meals from the grocery store, picnicking on moss-covered rocks and looking out at the murky yet beautiful ocean. I hiked ridiculously fast on local trails through volcanic boulder fields and luxuriated in the fact that no one was telling me I was doing too much or going too quickly. Alone and free, I found quirky, hidden art installations on mountaintops where I sang Bjork loudly to the empty landscape.

I had a total blast.

That trip to Iceland woke something that had lain dormant in me—a deep desire to be a solo adventurer far away from home. I wanted to learn the subtle teachings awaiting me on foreign shores. To immerse myself in other cultures and learn through profound listening. I desired to venture far from my comfort zone and meet the person I would find on the other side. And then, I wanted to figure out how to integrate that expanded version of myself when I returned home once again.

What Iceland had ignited, the Camino promised to build upon. I had walked the canyons of volcanic mountains. I had cried at the seashore from witnessing unrelenting beauty. I had awakened to desires in my heart and its special connection to the land. And now I felt ready to embrace a pilgrimage.

It is not easy to reach the starting point of the Camino Frances from the United States. For me, it necessitates a flight to Paris, a bus from the airport to the train station in Gare Montparnasse, a train ride to Bayonne, and then one final train transfer into Saint-Jean-Pied-de-Port. When I do arrive in town, I am feeling all the feels: excitement, dread, elation, regret. I observe fellow hikers exiting the train in twos and threes, checking maps to find their accommodations. Together, they create a communal buzz of anticipation for the journey ahead. Their camaraderie triggers my self-consciousness about being here alone, but these feelings quickly dissipate, as I am instantly distracted by the charm of the town, with its quaint cobblestone streets, historic homes, precariously stacked apartment buildings, and the colorful arrays of windowsill flowers. I immediately visit the Camino

headquarters to register as a pilgrim and get my credential passport, which I'll use to collect stamps from hostels and restaurants along the way to prove I made the full journey to Santiago de Compostela.

At the day's end, I purchase a scallop shell to tie to my backpack, which will identify me as a Camino pilgrim. There's a legend that when the body of Saint James was being transported from Jerusalem back to Spain, a mighty storm capsized the boat, and his body was seemingly lost to the ocean. However, it is said to have later miraculously washed ashore undamaged in Spain, covered in scallop shells. Thus the half shell became the sign of pilgrims making their own journey to Santiago de Compostela and is still worn by pilgrims today.

There's a commonly accepted philosophy around walking the Camino. They say that the journey can be separated into three stages. The first centers on your relationship with your body. Pilgrims spend an inordinate amount of time in their first week navigating the simplest of bodily needs, from finding food and lodging to dealing with blisters and aching muscles. The second stage of the Camino concerns your relationship with your mind and takes place in the Meseta, a 112-mile stretch of flat desert between Burgos and León. The mental challenge of being alone with your thoughts in this relatively featureless span of trail can be crushing. For some, the inner voice they work so hard to ignore in daily life is a bitter guest to host when those distractions fade away. Finally, the third stage of the Camino is associated with your relationship with God (or however you conceptualize your spirituality). After facing inner demons over long miles under open sky, you come to a point in the walk where spiritual expansion awaits. Going through these three stages is a highly personal process and manifests in radically different ways depending on the pilgrim. But the end results are often similar: a closer connection to the land around you, a deepened bond with something greater than yourself, and an individualized experience infused with spirituality.

The morning after my arrival in Saint-Jean-Pied-de-Port, I hastily leave my hotel and begin my walk. I immediately notice a similarly frenetic energy among my fellow pilgrims as we, for some unknown reason, seem to race each other out of town. It's as if we've forgotten that we have over a month to reach our destination! As soon as I begin walking, I am already awkwardly fumbling with the hiking poles I'd purchased for this walk (my first time ever using them). Fortunately, the kind owner of the outdoor-goods store next to my hotel approaches me and offers a quick lesson in their proper use. I am deeply grateful.

It does not take long after leaving town to find myself high in the Pyrenees Mountains. My pace is fast, and while I know it's barely sustainable, I feel this drive to reduce the distance between where I am and where I'm going. I still have 500 miles to go! The farther I get each day, I think, the quicker I can accomplish my goal of reaching

Santiago. The morning air is brisk, and the sun has only just risen. Shades of light in purples and pinks settle within the undulating lines of clouds grazing the horizon. It's only my first day, and already my Camino experience is exhilarating. I feel a deep sense of freedom as I walk, taking in the unfamiliar scenery and rejoicing in the feelings it awakens in me. I am really doing this. I am officially a pilgrim on the Camino Frances.

I continue walking quickly. Partly because I love the feeling of exertion in my body and partly because I am working hard to ensure that none of the other pilgrims will be able to keep up with me and thereby trap me in uncomfortable conversation. I'm the *worst* at small talk. In fact, being stuck conversing with strangers all day sounds downright torturous. And so, to avoid connecting with others, I walk fast and far beyond the recommended mileage, ending up alone in a hotel room a few towns over from where the guidebook says I should be.

My body is exhausted. And my heart is lonely.

That first night on the Camino, sitting by myself in a small hotel room, facing potentially thirty more days of complete isolation and quiet feels completely daunting. In some ways, this unexpected loneliness is so intense that it actually scares me, and I worry about being able to emotionally make it through an entire month completely on my own.

If the Rachel I am today could have a frank conversation with the Rachel in that room that night, I would tell her to pause and sit with the loneliness and discomfort. To send it some breath and tenderness. To be compassionate toward it and patient with its unfolding. And then I'd say to go downstairs to the hotel bar and make some damn friends.

But instead of employing any of these positive coping strategies to overcome my loneliness, I just try to override it.

My strategy to do so is simple. I'll walk as fast as possible. I'll talk to no one. I'll prove how strong I am, even though the loneliness feels like more weight on my already-overburdened back. I'll find comfort in my physical accomplishments, as opposed to forging personal connections. And I'll push through my emotions by focusing on what is happening on trail instead of what is unfolding in my heart.

Needless to say, my strategy doesn't work.

Not only does the loneliness persist, but a week into my kamikaze walking strategy, my shin begins to hurt, most likely from overuse. At first it's a slight discomfort. Nothing some compression sleeves, kinesiology tape, and large doses of Ibuprofen can't handle, I figure. But I notice that the more I walk, the more the pain intensifies. Even so, I refuse to slow down. I simply will not let any injury stand in the way of completing my pilgrimage.

Perhaps ironically, since my pain seems to be a consequence of hiking too fast in an attempt to isolate myself, the leg discomfort starts to emerge right as I finally make my first friend on trail. Lydia is simultaneously sweet and sassy, an ER doctor from Georgia who looks barely old enough to be out of college. I'd seen her on the trail before, hearing her effortless laughter as she walked with others. I envied how she could seamlessly connect so joyously to those around her. I coveted the way Lydia floated through conversations, delighting in opportunities to swap life stories and Camino ambitions. I had no idea how to approach her without seeming awkward or creepy but really hoped to find some way to say hello.

Our connection happens five days into the hike in a small town hosting a big celebration. As I stop to grab an Americano, a village elder approaches me and—using exaggerated hand gestures sprinkled with a few English words—invites me to the town hall for a party. There I find Lydia and a few of her friends enjoying free food and occasionally joining in the jovial dancing. I'm a practiced swing dancer, so it doesn't take me long to identify the local man with the best moves and ask him for a spin. We saunter dramatically around the small floor, sharing through our laughter and gestures what we can't express in words.

I leave the celebration with Lydia and her friends, and we continue walking as a group for the rest of the day. During those initial miles, we start to plant the seeds of what will become enduring friendships. For the next week, we cheer each other on and support each other emotionally through various Camino challenges: the lack of sleep due to snoring pilgrims in communal hostels, unwanted attention from men looking more for love than spiritual awakening, blistered feet and aching muscles, and waning motivation when the miles ahead seem interminable.

Together, we ease into the comforting balance of enjoying individual experiences within the wider support of a group. Though I still prefer walking alone during daylight hours, I enjoy coming together for our communal meals and sharing sessions at the end of each day. We compare the interesting stamps we received in our credentials. We share large *peregrino*, or pilgrim, meals, which include bread, three courses, and endless glasses of wine for only 10€ each. We laugh at the tribulations of the trail and rejoice in the accomplishments we have achieved. We become the Camino family I have been seeking.

Unfortunately, by the time our friendships grow sustainable roots, it is too late for me. I am seriously injured and feel that I have no choice but to abandon my Camino.

This heartbreaking realization happens on a beautiful day when the path takes us through a particularly stunning forest right outside the town of Burgos. I start off the morning walking solo, attempting to keep a decent pace. But as the hours pass, the agony in my leg becomes increasingly unbearable, and my shin struggles to hold my body's weight.

Eventually, I move off the trail into the forest and pass out from the pain. When I come to, still alone, I know my only option is to get somewhere with people and a phone to find help (the battery on my cell phone is dead). I have no choice: I grit my teeth through the pain as I slowly walk the next few miles, willing myself to take ten steps and then granting myself a break. Ten steps and then a break, repeated dozens of times. It takes hours, but ultimately, I make my way to a bar with a phone and find a cab to Burgos, the nearest large town.

I am hopeful that a few days of rest will have me back on trail. I find a physical therapist in town, and every day after our sessions, she has me place my leg in the freezing river that runs through the center of Burgos to ease the inflammation. I check into a lovely hotel and binge-watch episodes of *Unbreakable Kimmy Schmidt* and *Jane the Virgin* while I perform self-massage on my hurt leg.

And I pray.

Not to God, per se, or to the universe or to "Source," but to any entity that might listen and answer my prayer to get back on the Camino. I promise I'll do it differently this time. I'll listen to my body. I'll go slowly. I'll check my ego. I'll do whatever it takes.

But whatever higher power might be out there must have decided that I haven't fully learned my lesson because after four days of rest, I still can't walk without extreme pain. When I eventually talk to Lydia, who at that point is days ahead of me, she voices the truth of the situation that the PT didn't recognize and that I'd been terrified to hear—my leg is most likely fractured.

Somehow, I get myself back to the United States with only one working leg. Perhaps the lowest point of the journey home is my stay at the Madrid airport in a hotel room built ad hoc under an escalator. There is little more depressing than being alone in a windowless room underneath a moving walkway.

Once back in the US, I discover that my leg is indeed fractured. I am put into a shockingly large walking boot and told to rest for a month. I'm feeling both heartbroken and humiliated. I was supposed to return home triumphant after this month-long challenge. Instead, here I am in emotional pieces. I fully recognize that my injury is completely my fault. If I'd only just checked my ego and slowed down, I would have completed the journey.

But with time and some emotional work, I begin to see that there are multiple lessons and opportunities in every challenge. Being forced to rehab my leg gives me an opportunity to also rehab my mind and my heart. I use my time in therapy to explore why I felt the need to push so hard, avoid contact with strangers, and resist being present to the experience unfolding around me. I deepen my meditation practice and work on body awareness so I can be more clued in to what it is telling me instead of ignoring what it needs.

I create a healing support team. I get better shoes. I own up to what I could do differently. And I get better. I make a deal with myself before my planned return to the Camino four months later—that I'll stop every two hours for breaks. That I will not push through pain. That I will walk in a sustainable way and that I'll be open to making friends, even if it feels awkward.

Come September, it is time to put what I have learned into action.

I take the train from the Madrid airport to León and quickly find the first scallop-shell trail marker to show me the way. There's still a slight twinge of pain in my right leg that serves as a reminder to not mess this up again. Reinjury is a real possibility, and not completing this walk a second time would feel like the biggest failure of all. And so I pace myself. I find a sustainable gait. And I walk.

I can pretty much guarantee that no pilgrim walking through the industrial areas outside León's city center that day, with the ugly car parks and smoke-stacked factories, is experiencing anywhere close to the deep joy that I'm feeling. My gratitude for everything makes me feel almost buoyant. Being back is beyond delightful. I smile at everyone I pass. Every yellow arrow marking the way exhilarates me. Returning to the Camino is like the continuation of a song that my heart has been composing, and I'm grateful to finally be able to enjoy its sweet melody.

That evening, I even find myself sitting down with a group of strangers. And the next day, I strike up conversations when I stop for midday Americanos to rest my leg. When I feel the beginning pangs of loneliness on day three, instead of shoving them down, I listen to what my feelings signal and vow to form new connections. Just hours later, I pass a couple of college-aged walkers, one of whom is wearing a sweatshirt from Appalachian State University, just an hour away from where I live in Asheville! These fellow pilgrims soon form the nucleus of my new Camino family, which grows beautifully and organically as the days progress.

On my fourth day, I leave my mountain hut early to reach the Cruz de Ferro, one of the most important landmarks on the entire trail. With every step toward this magnificent monument, I imagine I'm ascending out of the person I had been when I walked this path four months earlier and settling into the person I am to become. The sun is just rising, and I see beauty everywhere. I am simultaneously on the land and yet also above it, melding earth and spirit with each step. And then, not far in the distance, I see the structure that I have been dreaming about. A striking metal cross towering more than twenty feet above the earth. Covering the ground at the foot of the cross are stones brought by pilgrims from around the world, as well as sacred objects and personal mementos. Tears well up in my eyes as I sit at the base of the cross and contemplate how far I've come to be at this place in this moment with this opportunity. The Camino has not rejected me as I'd previously felt. She simply wanted to make sure I was truly ready for the gifts she was willing to offer. I place the stone I have been saving for four months at the cross's base and, along with it, symbolically imagine leaving the struggles from my previous journey. My redemption moment is complete. I leave the mountaintop and continue on my two-week trek toward Santiago de Compostela.

The euphoria of those first few days stays with me for the rest of my time as a pilgrim. Surprisingly, I have transformed into someone who genuinely enjoys meeting new people. I strive to be fully present as I pass through the charming towns along the route. I eat freshly made bread from local bakeries, drink wine in cafes in village centers, and ask every establishment for their Camino stamp. I even occasionally opt to stay in communal hostels, even when there's a private hotel room available nearby.

And I make a family for myself. The group includes people from Spain, Australia, the US, Italy, and beyond. We look after each other. Together, we celebrate the completion of each day with lemon beers and endless laughter. We check in to make sure our needs are being met. And we help each other grow as both individuals and a community.

On our final day, the college couple and I wake before dawn and enter the forest outside Santiago de Compostela in full darkness. As we walk, it feels spookier than we anticipated, so we counter the creepiness by singing Madonna songs and trying to make each other laugh. When daylight finally fills the sky, we reach a hilltop that overlooks the sacred city of Santiago de Compostela, known as the city of stars. This place is the magnetic center of the Camino and the burial home of Saint James, the patron saint of Spain.

Words cannot capture what it feels like to see the spires of the cathedral materialize before my eyes. It's as if my heart is breaking a little so it can grow larger in size. I start crying heavily with the intensity of my contrasting emotions—deep grief for the trials of my journey and also overwhelming gratitude for making it to this moment. I have completed this quest, and yet I recognize that my process of learning through walking has just begun. I now know that I will forever be a pilgrim on life's trails. A seeker. A learner. Even when it is hard. Even when it is lonely. Even when I am frightened. Because I now understand that the most profound growth lies not in what I accomplish but within the journeys themselves. All I need to do is listen, allow, and walk.

LOGISTICS

Choosing a Route

The Camino Frances is a clearly established and marked route. Simply follow the yellow arrow blazes and scallop shells. That said, I found it helpful to refer to a Camino app on my phone to identify the route on the rare occasion the path was unclear. These apps work without cell service, provide distance to the nearest town, identify where you can find potable water fountains, and show available lodging. There are multiple apps to choose from, but I really enjoyed *The Wise Pilgrim*.

Getting to the Trailhead

The Camino Frances begins in Saint-Jean-Pied-de-Port on the French side of the Pyrenees. To get there, you can fly into Paris and take a high-speed train (TGV) to Bayonne. From Bayonne, take the mountain railway to Saint-Jean-Pied-de-Port. Once in town, there are clear markers to the start of the Camino.

Length and Difficulty

The Camino Frances is 491 miles long and is considered challenging. It takes between thirty and thirty-five days to walk.

Accommodations

There are two types of accommodations along the routes, *albergues* (public and private) and hotels. *Albergues* are communal hostels and often have mixed-gender rooms with bunk beds and shared bathrooms. Public *albergues* are usually run by the local municipality, are cheaper, and house many more people per room. These *albergues* are exclusively for pilgrims, and you have to show your credential to stay there. A credential is a Camino passport in which you collect stamps to prove you walked at least one hundred kilometers (just over sixty-two miles) of the route, which will entitle you to a certificate of completion in Santiago. Bedding is generally not included, but most public *albergues* sell a bedding set consisting of disposable sheets and a pillowcase for 1€.

Private *albergues* belong to a person or company and tend to offer nicer amenities. Space can be booked in advance by phone or through an online booking system. These *albergues* are not exclusively for pilgrims, though the majority of people staying there are usually walking the Camino. Both public and private *albergues* are plentiful along the path.

For a more private option, there are a variety of choices. Most towns along the Camino have hotels or other private (not dormitory) accommodations. These range in price and amenities and include, from the lowest cost to highest, simple *fondas* (rooms often offered by a local cafe/bar), *pensions* (simple rooms in local families' homes, sometimes with shared bathrooms), *hostales* (family-run hotels), hotels, and the more expensive *paradors* (restored historic buildings that have been converted into luxury hotels). Websites like Booking.com are helpful for finding private options.

Best Time to Hike

While the Camino is accessible year-round, the best times to hike are from April to June and September to October. I once hiked in May, which was quite rainy, and twice in September, when I had beautiful weather every day.

Pro Tips

One of the most delightful aspects of walking the Camino is collecting stamps from local restaurants and hotels. Each establishment along the Camino has its own unique stamp, so by the end of your journey, you'll have a lovely personalized memento of your time on trail. You can purchase your credential for 2€ at the pilgrim's office at the beginning of your hike or at tourist offices along the way. Make sure to get at least two stamps every day as proof of your journey.

Many restaurants along the Camino also provide specialty pilgrim meals from a *menu del peregrino*. This dine-in package deal includes bread, an appetizer, and a main course for around 10€. It also often includes unlimited regional wine! Finding pilgrim menus is a great way to keep costs down, enjoy local cuisine, and sustain restaurants committed to supporting pilgrims.

To avoid worrying about lodging, I recommend booking accommodations at least a few days ahead of time when possible. This will give you a sense of ease during the day since you won't have to rush to your end destination to find a room. And to make staying in *albergues* more enjoyable, there are a few small things I recommend bringing that will make a world of difference. Make sure you have high-quality earplugs as you will most likely share space with some alarmingly loud snorers. Also, bring a good sleeping mask to make it easier to sleep whether or not the lights are on. A quick-dry travel towel is a must. I also recommend bringing some lightweight string and clothespins for hanging laundry. And Dr. Bronner's Pure-Castile Liquid Soap is perfect for travel because you can use it for your body, laundry, and doing dishes!

But if I could recommend one thing above all others, it would be to wear trail runners on the Camino (and all hikes, for that matter). There is absolutely no need to wear hiking boots. In fact, those who wear hiking boots tend to suffer the worst blisters and muscle strains. I saw many pilgrims abandoning their expensive hiking boots for sneakers they'd bought locally. And on a related note, taking care of your feet is your top priority. As soon as you feel a hot spot, take the time to remove your shoe and apply a Compeed Anti-Blister Patch, which are available at pharmacies all along the Camino.

And remember, the heavier your pack, the less enjoyable your experience will be. Make sure you bring only the essentials: two pairs of hiking shorts or pants, two pairs of underwear, two pairs of socks and sock liners, two hiking T-shirts, a warmer long-sleeved shirt, something to sleep in, and a hat should be plenty. If you know someone who has walked the Camino, ask if they will go through your pack to help you pare it down to only what's absolutely necessary. Anything else you may need can be purchased in towns along the way.

BOOKS

A Pilgrim's Guide to the Camino de Santiago (Camino Frances): St. Jean Pied de Port to Santiago de Compostela by John Brierley (Findhorn Press).

The Art of Pilgrimage: The Seeker's Guide to Making Travel Sacred by Phil Cousineau and Huston Smith (Conari Press).

One of the aspects of Brierley's book I really appreciated is that it provides alternative routes that will take you on more beautiful, less populated trails. Every day, I would tear out that day's description to carry in my pocket so it was easy to reference.

LOCAL LANGUAGE: SPANISH

Thank you: Gracias (GRAH-sea-ahs)
Please: Por favor (pour FAH-vor)
I'm sorry: Lo siento (low SEA-en-toe)

REGIONAL RECIPE

Patatas Bravas is a delicious delicacy served in almost every restaurant on the Camino. Traditionally, the potatoes are fried, but this is a healthier baked version.

PATATAS BRAVAS

Serves 4

INGREDIENTS

For the potatoes

2 pounds Yukon or red potatoes, cut into bite-size pieces

1–2 tbsp olive oil

1 generous pinch sea salt

1 generous pinch garlic powder

For the sauce

1 tbsp olive oil

½ white or yellow onion, diced

5 garlic cloves, minced

½ tsp sea salt

½ tsp paprika

1 pinch cayenne or red pepper flakes

1 (6 oz) can tomato paste

2–3 tsp hot sauce

1½ cups water

For a spicier sauce, add a few extra dashes of hot sauce or more chili flakes.

DIRECTIONS

1. Preheat the oven to 450°F. Soak potatoes in very hot water for 10–15 minutes.

2. Once potatoes are soaked, pat dry thoroughly and add to a baking sheet with 1–2 tbsp of olive oil and generous sprinkling of sea salt and garlic powder. Toss to coat.

3. Bake for 20–25 minutes or until golden brown and cooked through, stirring/tossing once. Test by spearing a potato with a toothpick—it should be easy to pierce.

4. While potatoes are baking, prepare spicy tomato sauce. Heat 1 tbsp of olive oil in a large skillet over medium-low heat. Add onion, garlic, and salt and stir.

5. Cook for 7–8 minutes to slowly "sweat" until the mixture becomes translucent and very fragrant. If it begins to brown, turn down the heat to low and stir frequently.

6. Add paprika, garlic powder, and cayenne and stir.

7. Add tomato paste, hot sauce, and water and stir.

8. Cook on medium heat for 10–12 minutes or until mixture is simmering and flavors are well blended. Reduce heat if it begins to bubble too vigorously. Taste and adjust seasonings as needed.

9. For a smooth sauce, purée in a small blender or food processor.

10. Remove potatoes from the oven and sprinkle with a bit more salt to taste. Place in a serving dish and drizzle with sauce.

Everest Base Camp

March 2017

DIFFICULTY: Strenuous | **LENGTH: 39 miles (79 km)** | **ELEVATION GAIN: 8,215 feet (2,503 m)** | **DURATION: 12–15 days**

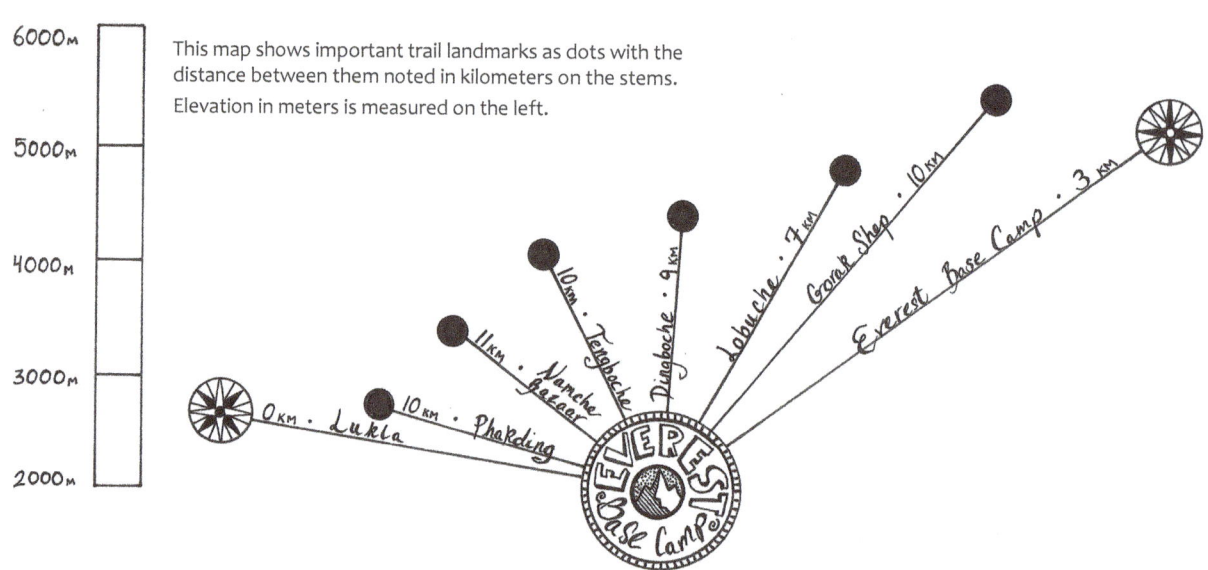

This map shows important trail landmarks as dots with the distance between them noted in kilometers on the stems. Elevation in meters is measured on the left.

Hiking is not escapism; it's realism.
The people who choose to spend time outdoors
are not running away from anything;
we are returning to where we belong.

—JENNIFER PHARR DAVIS

The clock on my phone shines three o'clock in the morning. I am lying on a rigid bed consisting of only a thin mattress laid over a single piece of plywood. My room is on the top floor of a teahouse, the Nepalese equivalent of a mountain hut, at more than 16,000 feet above sea level. The temperature inside is shockingly cold, and my muscles are stiff and sore due to a severe lack of oxygen. Breathing is a labored exercise even when lying down, and when I'm not focusing on my breath, my attention moves to my distended stomach, which makes me look four months pregnant.

Altitude is a real bitch.

But despite the cold and discomfort and the fact that I barely slept (plywood walls being effective for neither sound nor heat insulation), I am wide awake and ready for the challenge ahead. And a challenge it will certainly be. The weather outside is below freezing. I know that even the multiple down jackets and layers of fleece I'm wearing will not stand a chance against the biting wind and bone-chilling temperatures here in the highlands of Nepal. And yet—surprisingly—the cold is the least of my worries. With more than 2,000 feet of vertical ascent ahead of me, I am about to face the impact of altitude on my body at a shockingly intense level.

Memories of my ascent of Kilimanjaro (at more than 19,000 feet tall) six years earlier flash in my mind. The crippling pain I'd felt in every muscle as I somehow found the will to push myself up the mountain. The way my breath seemed to barely reach my lungs, making each inhale feel like a fight for survival. My frozen water bottle mocking my dehydrated state. And the constant sense of disorientation and exhaustion that made a successful summit feel nothing less than impossible (though, somehow, I made it in the end).

Lying in my room in Nepal, I realize that all these same challenges lie between me and the top of Kala Patthar, standing at 18,519 feet. But knowing there will be no reward of seeing the sun rising over Everest's peak if there is no imposing hike to conquer, I prepare myself to attempt one of the most significant summits I will achieve in my lifetime. I pull myself out of my **0**-degree sleeping bag, put on every layer of clothing I brought with me, and go outside to join my group for the final push of our trek.

It is the twelfth day of our journey through the mountains of the Khumbu region. I began this trip in the dusty, bustling city of Kathmandu as my fellow adventurer Emily (an eighteen-year-old from Connecticut who was the only other person signed up for our expedition) and I absorbed the sights, smells, and sounds of Nepal. As we walked among ancient buildings and along winding alleyways, our senses were delighted by the aromatic scent of sizzling lentils from outdoor food carts, displays of brightly colored saris in store windows, and the repetitive chanting of Buddhist mantras emerging from booming speaker systems.

At the start of our journey, Emily is quiet and hard to read. At our first breakfast together, we have an extraordinarily awkward conversation with long, painful pauses. I have thirty-nine years to her eighteen, and try as I might, I do not know how to bridge the gap between our different generational worldviews. I am apprehensive about fifteen days on trail together. But fortunately, a few days into our adventure, our time together on trail, our collective experience pushing through intense physical challenges, and our mutual appreciation of french fries ends up creating a connection and a friendship that have lasted for years.

To begin the trek to Everest Base Camp, you have to travel to the small mountain town of Lukla. How does one capture what it is like to fly from Kathmandu to Lukla, known for the world's most dangerous airport runway? If you can imagine every potential problem an airport might have, Lukla has it in spades. Its runway is shockingly short at a mere 1,729 feet (for comparison's sake, the average commercial runway is 8,000–13,000 feet) and ends at a sharp right angle, where planes only just avert crashing into the mountainside. To make things even more challenging, the mountainous region surrounding Lukla generates its own wind patterns and flight hazards, and the high altitude creates a low-pressure pocket that can wreak havoc on a plane's stability. The flight into Lukla is legendary in its capacity to terrify and nauseate even the most seasoned of Everest guides. I spend hours the night before our scheduled departure practicing deep breathing and wondering if 5:00 a.m. is too early for a stiff shot of whiskey to ease my nerves.

Not to be outdone, the Kathmandu airport has its own challenges. Its mood brings to mind a big-box store the day after Thanksgiving, and "chaos" is too tame to capture the unbounded madness. First, everyone's bag must be weighed before you even enter the airport, so there's an initial frenzy to pass through bag inspection to reach the terminal. Once inside, confused hikers searching for their specific chartered flights swarm the airline counters, so by the time we finally check in and arrive at the gate (filled with what feels like thousands of people), I sense a mix of high anxiety and overwhelming anticipation. And after all that, our departure isn't even guaranteed. If we are able to take off at all, there'll be only a small window of opportunity when the weather around Everest clears enough for us to jump on a plane and make the thirty-minute journey around the world's highest peak to Lukla's miniscule landing strip. If the perfect conditions do not coalesce, we will have to wait and try again the next day, repeating the entire maddening process.

After a couple of hours, we get the "go" signal, and all the waiting passengers descend to the runway and fling themselves into their assigned planes. Emily and I take the first available seats and secure ourselves with a multilevel seat-belt system. I have no idea if my bags are on this plane. I have no idea if I am even on the right airline. But there is nothing we can do now. Emily and I exchange terrified looks as we suddenly lift into the air and are on our way.

Fortunately, our flight and arrival are mostly uneventful, apart from the unbelievable landscape that surrounds us. Mountain peaks encased in snow jut thousands of feet above the ground. Their picturesque configurations both invite and intimidate me, and I immediately feel an immense reverence for this place and for what I am about to do.

It takes a couple of days of hiking for us to reach the first mountain town. The emerald valleys we pass through contrast harshly against some of the world's highest peaks towering above. The trail is worn and yet surrounded by lushness: the lush greenery, the lush scents of Nepalese food, and the lush colors of the small homes dotting the countryside.

At the start of our journey, I am most struck by the abundant and beautiful prayer stones. These colorful rocks decorate the trail and landscape throughout the region and appear in all sizes and shapes, from solitary palm-size stones on limestone pedestals to entire boulders that occupy a mountain's edge. They honor the sacredness of the land and are a physical symbol of the dedication of the thousands of pilgrims who have walked the peaks and valleys of the Khumbu region. Prayer stones are either carved or painted and display the sacred Buddhist mantra *"om mani padme hum."* Translating loosely to "praise to the jewel in the lotus," this most holy of Buddhist chants is said to protect those who pass and serves as a reminder of the vital role of kindness and wisdom along the path to enlightenment.

Even high in the stony mountains, Nepal is a celebration of color. As our hike progresses, we are greeted with thousands of prayer flags placed precariously on bridges and in treetops. From there, the wind can carry their intentions to the gods, who are believed to live among the tallest peaks. As I hike, I feel the power of the mountain infused with the dreams, wishes, and heart songs of those who have walked this land for thousands of years. Our steps traverse the sacred line where human and mountain, spirit and land, meet.

When we reach the town of Namche on the second day, the relative silence of the mountain path gives way to the discordant sounds and sights of the local bazaar where vendors are selling everything from food and hiking gear to Everest-themed beer. The stalls are framed by the colorful backdrop of houses and tea huts lining the mountain terraces. The combination of colors, food smells, and the sounds of hikers chatting in a multitude of languages makes my every sense go gloriously into overdrive, and I delight in the chaos of it all.

In Namche, it really feels like we are here to climb.

Our accommodation at the teahouse that evening is simple—Pepto Bismol-colored walls, plywood beds, and no hot water. But the restaurant is top-notch, and their *momos* (Nepalese dumplings) are the best I have ever had. It is these scrumptious *momos* that, weeks later, will motivate me to crush the extra miles and finish our hike a day early, just so we can return to this very restaurant to savor their delicious, warm comfort once again.

After dinner, my anxiety about the journey ahead sets in because once we leave this town, we will truly be in the remote backcountry of Nepal. After Namche, should there be a serious injury or illness, the only way out is by helicopter evacuation. This is when things get real and when a new level of the adventure begins. Unfortunately, Emily is already suffering from altitude sickness, which can happen when you ascend too rapidly, and your body does not have enough time to adjust to the reduced oxygen. It appears to choose its victims at random, with no correlation to health or fitness. There is some discussion about whether or not she will be able to continue on. Already her face is pale and scarily inflamed, and her speech is noticeably slurred. She is struggling, but she is determined. When the leaders of our hike check in with her, she blatantly refuses to abort the journey, and I see that no amount of dizziness or stomach upset is going to prevent this fighter from reaching the base of Mount Everest. Perhaps against the guides' better judgment, Emily and I set off with our team the next day.

As we walk, we begin to deepen our connection with our guides Kale (KAH-lee) and Manish (MAH-neesh). Kale has led hikes on this mountain for decades and has a kind and easy manner, with a sense of humor that fluctuates between charming and corny. Manish is just in his early twenties and is shy and delightfully awkward as he moves his large body swiftly up and down the trail. I was warned during orientation that Manish was

the stoic, silent type and that I could expect expertise in regard to safety and skills from him but not any meaningful type of connection.

Thankfully, my orientation presenter was quite wrong.

I instantly adore Manish. We connect easily, even though the only three things we can identify in common are our love of Marvel movies, hiking, and Nepalese dumplings.

The words we exchange are few, but our energy syncs up in a symbiotic harmony. We race each other up mountain passes and cheer each other on as we cautiously walk over suspension bridges whose very existence seems to challenge the laws of physics. We laugh at each other's quirky facial expressions, which quickly become our secret language. And we honor shared silences when the majesty of the mountains demands that we pause and offer veneration.

The four of us quickly transform from awkward strangers to a synergistic team of determined hikers, and for two weeks, we work together to push through freezing temperatures, low oxygen, dangerous passes, potentially angry yaks, and unrelenting uphill ascents to reach the base of the most famous mountain in the world.

The scene as we approach Base Camp is oddly not what I had expected. Unlike other hikes whose grand finale is preceded by a steep uphill push, the final few miles to the base of Everest are flat and lack climactic flair. We walk this last section together, traveling among formidable ice and snow formations, until we see a village of orange and yellow tents ahead. Prayer flags placed by people from around the world decorate the mountain's base, and when we reach the officially designated spot, we pose joyously for photos with the grandeur of Everest as the backdrop. Never one to miss an opportunity for a spiritual moment, I walk away from our group to find a quiet enclave and sit in silent reverence before the mountain, allowing the deep, earthly, energetic vibrations to imprint on my mind and on my heart.

But Base Camp is just a part of our journey's end goal. The true anticipated moment will occur the next morning, when we rise before dawn to climb the steep spine of Kala Patthar to its 18,519-foot summit (to put that in perspective, that is about the height of fifty-one football fields placed vertically, end to end). Once there, we will sit and watch as the sun slowly climbs its way out of the snowy, dark depths of night to gently illuminate the slick granite silhouette of Mount Everest.

As we begin our ascent early the next morning, I am surprised to find the air slightly warmer than anticipated, so I quickly shed some of my bulkier layers to hike comfortably in only two pairs of long underwear, fleece pants, hiking pants, a fleece sweater, and one down jacket. The trail starts out with a gentle flatness for which I am grateful because the moment the trajectory starts going uphill, everything gets hard for me. Breathing becomes a struggle with access to only half the oxygen available at sea level. My muscles are screaming with pain. Each step is a battle of deciding whether I can win this mental game over my physical limitations and make it to the top of the mountain.

Though I felt the effect of altitude about four days into our trip, resulting in a distended stomach and diminished appetite, this is an entirely different experience. The pain and discomfort are next level. With Emily hiking separately behind me, I can only hope she is able to overcome altitude's harm enough to make it to the top. It takes several unpleasant hours to push myself up to Kala Patthar's summit. I spend my mental energy cursing myself for choosing another altitude hike after the suffering I felt on Kilimanjaro. I abhor every loose pebble and strewn rock that threaten to rotate my ankle and cause a sprain. And I become acutely aware of places in my body where I did not realize pain was possible. But for me there is no other option than up. And so I push on.

They say the ascent just before the summit is always the steepest, and as the incline becomes almost unbearable, I try to console myself that I must be close—that all this suffering will be worth it, and the promise of a sunrise is near. And then, somehow, I arrive. Exhausted, I sit down on the mountain's east-facing slope and turn to see, almost in disbelief, the triangular top of Mount Everest 11,000 feet above me. Next to me, a fellow hiker shivers with cold. I give him my hand warmers and congratulate him on his ascent as we both turn to notice the first glimmer of yellow daylight break through the early-morning blackness.

Everest looks almost like an ancient pyramid as the promise of dawn traces its silhouette against the milky gray of the rapidly transforming sky. I am utterly speechless. It feels like the magnitude of everything I am witnessing has tunneled into an unexplored spiritual depth inside me. Something in my heart shifts. I lose all sense of individuality and meld into mountain, stone, air.

The mountainside quickly empties of cold, tired hikers, but I stay where I am long after the sun has peaked above the towering mountain. Long after morning birdsong begins to fill the air. Long after I can no longer feel my fingers and toes. I stay because I recognize in this moment access to a wisdom and an energy unique in all the world. I fear moving because I do not want to lose this connection that expands beyond body and into something much bigger than what my mind can comprehend. I am simultaneously humbled, enlivened, peaceful, and exhausted. Eventually I absorb all I can. I thank the mountain one final time, and begin the awaiting long descent.

LOGISTICS

There are three ways you can hike from Lukla to the base of Mount Everest. The first (and the one I chose) is with an organized tour. The benefit of this choice is that everything is arranged for you, including permits, porters, and meals. You also have the advantage of working with local guides who provide insider knowledge about the region and can help with safety preparedness, as well as addressing any challenges encountered on trail. The second option is to arrive at Kathmandu and hire a local guide and porter to accompany you on the trek. Finally, you can hike unaccompanied, but this requires a lot more planning and a high level of trail competence.

For more in-depth information, the website Stingy Nomads is a fantastic resource for route options to Base Camp.

Getting to the Trailhead

Travelers should plan to initially arrive in Kathmandu, Nepal's capital city. I suggest spending a few days there to overcome jet lag and to take in the city's beautiful historic sites, such as hiking to Swayambhunath Stupa, visiting the Pashupatinath Temple, and exploring the Boudhanath Stupa. From Kathmandu, you will fly to Lukla. It's a good idea to have a few days of flexibility in your schedule since flights are frequently canceled due to weather. You can stay overnight in Lukla or begin trekking the day you arrive.

Length and Difficulty

For many, the most challenging aspect of hiking to Base Camp is dealing with altitude sickness to varying degrees. Though there are significant gains in elevation on the trail, you do not need any specific technical skills, and a moderate level of fitness is sufficient to complete the hike.

Trekking from Lukla to Base Camp typically takes from twelve to fifteen days, which includes a few days for acclimatization. You will cover thirty-nine miles and gain almost 8,215 feet of elevation.

Accommodations

Small, minimalist mountain huts known as teahouses provide overnight shelter along the trail. They often do not have running water or heat but do offer rudimentary beds and drop toilets. They also provide food served in basic restaurants.

Best Time to Hike

March to May and October to November are the best months to trek in the Himalayas of Nepal. In spring, the rhododendrons are in bloom along the trails. After spring, the monsoon season picks up, and you can expect daily rain from June through September.

Pro Tips

My most emphatic recommendation is to eat as many *momos* as possible. Even just thinking about *momos* makes my heart happy. Outside of that, if you have not read *Into Thin Air* by Jon Krakauer, definitely *wait* to do so until you get back home so as not to become frightened of the trek. If you suffer from motion sickness, bring Dramamine for the flight into Lukla. And do not skimp on warm clothes. It gets seriously cold in those mountains.

I also highly recommend taking Diamox, a prescription-based altitude-sickness pill. Though it will give you crazy dreams and make you pee a lot, it might also save your life at high elevation. Natural remedies that can also help with altitude include coca-leaf tea and chlorophyll pills.

Finally, I urge you to watch a powerful film called *Sherpa* that addresses some of the abuses that sherpas (i.e., local guides and porters) face while supporting Western hikers on the mountain. Watch the film before you go, and if you choose to hike with a guided tour, ask the company what they do to protect the well-being of their staff.

BOOKS

Trekking Everest: Base Camp, Kala Patar and Other Trekking Routes in Nepal and Tibet (Cicerone Trekking Guides) by Kev Reynolds.

LOCAL LANGUAGE: NEPALI

Thank you: धन्यवाद (dhanya-BAAD)
Please: कृपया (KREE-pay-ah)
I'm sorry: म दुःखी छु। (MA-du chi-chu)

REGIONAL RECIPE

Nothing made me happier on trail than eating *momos*. Enjoy this vegan version!

VEGETARIAN MOMOS
(Traditional Tibetan Dumplings)

Serves 4

INGREDIENTS

For the dough

2½ cups all-purpose flour

1½ cups water

pinch of salt

For the filling

oil, as needed

1 tsp finely chopped garlic

½ cup finely chopped yellow onion

1 cup finely chopped green cabbage

1 cup finely chopped bell pepper

1 cup finely chopped carrot

1 tsp black pepper

salt to taste

DIRECTIONS

For the dough

Mix flour, water, and salt in a bowl to create dough. It should be slightly rubbery and not too watery. Set dough aside to rest while you make the filling.

For the filling

1. Heat some oil in a pan; when it's hot, add garlic and let it cook for about 2 minutes.

2. Add onions and sauté mixture for 2 minutes until it turns golden brown.

3. Add cabbage, bell pepper, and carrot to mixture. Stir fry the vegetables and add black pepper and salt.

4. Let mixture cook for 5–7 minutes and set aside.

PREPARING THE MOMOS

1. Make small balls (about 2–3 inches) from the dough.

2. On a floured surface, roll each ball into a small circle. The size of each circle should be around 3–4 inches in diameter. I recommend dipping the bottom of a glass in water and using the dampened glass to flatten the dough balls. Make sure there is still some thickness to the dough so it can hold the filling.

3. Place some filling in the center of each circle (about 1 tbsp).

4. Fold the circle in half to bring the edges together to seal the dumpling. Make sure the filling doesn't come out.

5. Heat water in a steamer. Once water is heated, place the momos inside. Let them steam for about 10 minutes.

6. When the momo dough is soft, they are done. Serve piping hot with pepper sauce or momo chutneyWhen the momo dough is soft, they are done. Serve piping hot with sauce or chutney.

Aniakchak Crater

July 2017

DIFFICULTY: Strenuous | LENGTH: **~100 miles (161 km)** | ELEVATION GAIN: **10,000 feet (3,048 m)** | DURATION: **11 days**

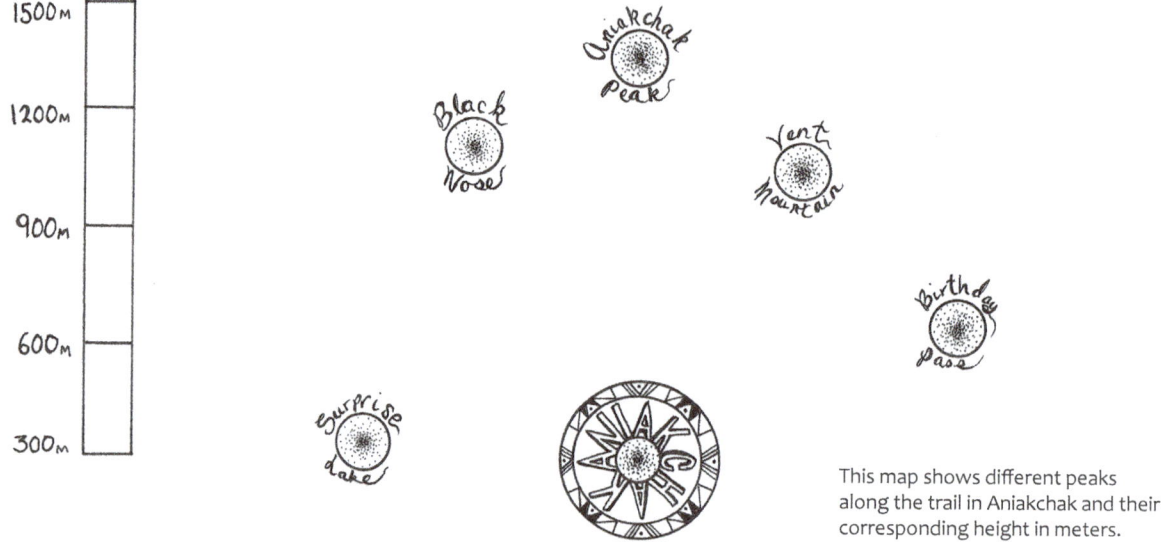

This map shows different peaks along the trail in Aniakchak and their corresponding height in meters.

Life is either a daring adventure or nothing.

—HELEN KELLER

 LESSON... **You are stronger than you think.**

Generally speaking, I try to find the positive in what could be perceived as a negative experience. Example: had I not injured myself on my first Camino, I would not have been home in May of 2016 for my friend Drew's "bring an instrument and see what happens" party. And had I not put on my big-girl pants, forcing myself to overcome both my own intense shyness and seriously mediocre ukulele playing, I would not have crossed paths with a man named Kenan at said party.

Kenan is a serious hiker whose intense sense of trail adventure transforms the promise of adversity into the delight of opportunity. No trail is too hard, no weather too treacherous, no challenge too out of bounds. Kenan is fearless, and he is just the type of trekker who will ultimately push me out of my comfort zone and show me what I am truly capable of on trail.

That ragtag musicians' jam at Drew's eventually led to the creation of a three-piece Cure cover band called "The Cure Alls." Drew held the beat on rhythm guitar, Kenan replaced the sounds of synthesized pop with an electric fiddle, and I interpreted Robert Smith's emotive vocals as soulful renditions of his New Wave masterpieces. Over the years, our band has had exactly zero public performances, has rehearsed at most three times annually, and still has only five songs in our repertoire. But though our outward successes are few, it is always pure joy when we do get together and play.

At our first band session, I had just returned from hiking to the base of Mount Everest. Something in rehearsal sparked a memory from my trip, and as I began to share a quirky anecdote about the hike I noticed that Kenan's focus on what I was saying had become razor sharp. "It sounds like you enjoy doing some pretty intense and crazy hiking," he said. I responded that I enjoyed a good challenge and a great view, but I was not quite sure what he meant by "crazy."

Little did I know then that in a few months, I would find out.

Kenan became animated as he began to talk about Aniakchak, an eleven–day loop hike in an active volcano on Alaska's Aleutian Peninsula. He'd read about it in *Outside* magazine and became instantly obsessed. Could he share the article with me and see if it resonated?

Absolutely.

The article, titled "Baked Alaska: Surviving Aniakchak National Monument," opens with these words: "The volcanic remains at the heart of Aniakchak National

Monument—the least visited site in the National Park system—are a trippy mishmash of post apocalyptic cinder cones, hardened lava, and flame-colored walls. The only catch? Doing it right involves days of trekking and rafting through some of the planet's toughest, most bear-heavy terrain."

The rest of the article was peppered with phrases like "man-eating vegetables," "alder jungles that swallow bushwhackers," "cow parsnip with poison leaves that blister the skin," "unrelenting storms," "not a single marked trail," and wolves in "packs of 40."

I called Kenan immediately and decisively told him no.

"But aren't you a little curious?" he responded. "Didn't reading the article spark something faint within you that feels a little bit like a calling?"

Unlike my new friend, I did not feel even remotely "called" to hike without marked trails in wretched weather conditions. Though I am always up for a physical challenge, the idea of being soaked by powerful storms while bushwhacking through poisonous plants in grizzly country not only held zero appeal for me, it sounded oppressive.

A few days later, however, I found myself rereading the article. Having moved past my initial shock at the harsh conditions it described, I was pulled in by some of the other characteristics of Aniakchak: the chance to hike into the caldera of an active volcano, the opportunity to see neon-green lakes and orange thermal rivers carved through the volcanic landscape, and the challenge of hiking up lava-spill formations to marvel at the crater-filled, otherworldly landscape below.

But my answer for Kenan was still no.

It remained no when I read the article a third time and then a fourth. But the no that was so firm at first was beginning to weaken. My feelings about the hike developed a porousness that expanded until a slight essence of "yes" took root. I knew it was unlikely to be the most enjoyable hike of my life, but Aniakchak was calling, and I could not turn away from the beckoning of her voice.

"Let's do it," I told Kenan as he picked up the phone—most likely prepared for me to start rattling off yet again all the reasons why this hike was a terrible idea. He was silent for a couple of beats, and then, even though I could not see him, I felt his smile begin to grow on the other end of the call.

It turns out that Kenan is an extraordinary travel companion. He is funny and adventurous and loves talking to random strangers (a personality trait I admire and very much lack). As we begin our trip, his extrovert nature beautifully rounds out my introvert tendencies as we navigate canceled planes in Chicago, missed connections in Seattle, and a stay in a quirky Anchorage hotel. By the time we meet up with the other two members of our tour group in Anchorage, we have happily and smoothly transitioned from acquaintances to fast friends.

The only other person who willingly signed up to hike Aniakchak is a recent college graduate whose name also happens to be Emily. She is tall and of slight build and has fabulous lavender hair. And then there is our guide, John. He is a legend in the Alaskan outback, having pioneered trekking through some of the harshest and uncharted territories in the state. John is quiet and understated, and given his track record, I trust him to be the best of the best to take us where very few have gone before.

To give an idea of how remote (or perhaps unappealing) Aniakchak is, 9.7 million people visited the Great Smoky Mountains National Park in 2012, making it the busiest national park in the country. That same year, nineteen people made the journey to Aniakchak.

Just nineteen.

On day two of our adventure, we are transported to the park by float plane. At our final gear check the night before, my bag was even heavier than anticipated, loaded with necessary gear and food—and at the airport weigh-in, it's a whopping fifty-four pounds. I have *never* carried anything close to that heavy on a hike. After I load my pack on the plane for our hour-long ride, I place my palms on my lap and say a silent prayer that my legs are ready for the challenge ahead.

We land in the clouds, a thick, soupy fog creating a shroud of invisibility. As the pilot removes our packs from the plane's cargo container, he expresses genuine shock that we are going to carry these monstrosities for the next eleven days. This does nothing for my confidence, and I turn to John for reassurance, but he simply hands me a can of bear spray while keeping his head down, seeing to last-minute preparations. By the time we put on our packs, the plane's propeller has started to turn, and we watch as the aircraft begins its ascent back to Anchorage. There is no turning back now. The four of us begin to walk.

The first part of our trek follows an old ATV trail through the foliage. The outline of the path is faint at best, but at least it provides some idea of where we are headed. An amber-colored fox greets us near the beginning of the trail, and I decide that this is an auspicious sign for the hike ahead. But still, those first four miles are brutal. I spend much of my energy fighting my way through prickly plants I can't identify. Mosquitoes buzz noisily around our heads, and I quickly grab my head net and gloves to protect any remaining exposed skin from their merciless predation.

It does not take long for me to decide that I have, without a doubt, made a terrible mistake by coming here.

Eventually, we find a clearing within the sopping brush we've been pushing through for the past three hours. It's flat enough for our four tents, but I find our surroundings immensely depressing. The thick fog feels pregnant with rain that might fall on us at any moment, and the ground is pockmarked with ATV tracks that have solidified into deep muddy trenches. It's almost a complete whiteout, so anything that might be considered beautiful is fully obscured. My heart feels heavy, leaning dangerously close to defeated. It can only get better from here, I think as I set up my borrowed one-person tent, which is barely bigger than my sleeping bag. Inside, I slowly begin stripping off my soaked clothes, which I am pretty sure will not dry before the end of the trip, and search for warmer layers at the bottom of my pack.

As we make dinner under the shelter of a tarp, my mood is dark. I am cold. It is ugly here. All I can see is gray and the occasional piece of litter left by an ATV adventurer. I have quickly become aware that a hefty dose of misery will likely infuse most of my experience in the Alaskan outback. When it's finally time for bed, I cuddle into my 0-degree bag and do my best not to cry or panic (both feel surprisingly hard to resist). I send every ounce of energy into the hope of tomorrow being a better day.

When morning comes, I begrudgingly leave the warmth of my tent to join the others for breakfast. The grayness of the day before has thankfully lifted, and the increased visibility raises my spirits. The air is cool, but the sun has reclaimed its space in the sky.

Today we begin to climb.

Since there are no trails in the park, and John has never hiked in this area before, we do not—and cannot—know the elevation gain or exact mileage awaiting us. Everything in front of us is a game of "best guess," which makes this feel like an adventure unique unto itself. I find it surprisingly hard to settle into the hike with nothing but unknowns lining our way, and already I can tell this journey is going to be much more about mental fortitude than physical strength.

Leaving camp is an uphill slog. The terrain is packed with calf-high dirt mounds that are impossible to avoid, and so it feels like I'm carrying a fifty-pound suitcase up and down a large step, over and over and over. The repetition and uneven terrain are close to maddening, and my thoughts get stuck on how miserable I am. Since we have not yet honed our group communication skills, I realize later in the day that the three of us are assuming that the others want to go faster than we actually do individually, and so we spend the first few hours exhausting ourselves. Finally, the hurt in my body drowns out my ego, and I call it, which is gratefully greeted with deep sighs of relief from everyone else. Happy to know that I am not going to spend the entire trip attempting to jog up and down mountains while carrying a fifty-pound pack, I sink into a more dignified stride and continue the up-and-down routine until we reach camp that night.

Though the hike is only slightly more enjoyable that second day, the group is beginning to coalesce and connect. Emily is a dedicated vegan, and we spend hours trading recipe ideas and discussing the ethics that inspired our choice to embrace a plant-based lifestyle. We swap the names of our favorite cruelty-free products and promise to email each other cookbook recommendations when we return home. Kenan and John seem to connect effortlessly, and the few times I pass them, they are sharing trail love stories that celebrate the challenges and relish the adventure.

Our best moment during the second day is coming across a herd of caribou. After cresting a hill that leads to an open meadow, we are greeted with the sight of these magnificent creatures lining the hillside. John tells us to get low so as to not scare them, and we lie on the soft, moss-covered ground in silence to watch them move gracefully through the short grass. Their elegant frames are beautifully silhouetted against a sky of gray and blue. John informs us that if we hold our hiking poles like antlers on the tops of our heads, the caribou will not be able to distinguish us from their own kind. I'm not sure if this is just a way to make us look ridiculous, but I hesitantly raise my metal poles into an antler-like position above my head and awkwardly look up. The caribou immediately cease their activities and silently observe us just as we are observing them.

Seeing a solitary animal in the wild is always an exhilarating experience, but seeing this herd of caribou feels otherworldly. Without trees to create texture against the landscape, the animals are the sole visual interruption in the sea of undulating green grass. We sit there, poles on heads, for many slow-moving minutes until the animals silently indicate to each other that it's time to gather and move. Even after the herd's departure, we remain transfixed by the energy left in the wake of their migration.

I sleep really well that night.

By day four, I resign myself to the discomforts of the trail. Though I do not enjoy it, I become accustomed to the cold and mist that envelop everything. I hone my tactics to avoid the swarms of mosquitoes whose tenacity for blood is almost admirable. I bring my best mindfulness skills to try to appreciate the lack of variation in the landscape, creating fun mental games to distract myself from the monotony of the unrelenting uphill climbs. I even find some peaceful acceptance around the fact that we need to stay together as a group for safety, which unfortunately, eliminates my precious alone time. What I feel less grace around is my relationship to my pack, which I name Esther after one of my spiritual teachers. The pain on my hips as fifty-four pounds push into my pelvic bones never gets easier to bear, and as the days wear on, the pressure etches grooves into my skin.

And yet, on that fourth day of hiking, I also start to find a bit more joy in our situation. Little things begin to raise my spirits. I notice beauty in the way crystal-clear mountain streams carve winding pathways through the greenery of the hillsides. I take

in the vastness of the landscape and how it distorts distance and height with its disorientating lack of perspective. I appreciate the way the four of us have become a unit as we cover unfamiliar land, overcoming the unending challenges that the Alaskan wilderness presents. Most importantly, I love discovering the new ways my body is strong and capable and adept, which I would not have realized had my feet never touched this land.

By day five, I find my rhythm. I wake up in the morning shuddering from the cold and quickly bundle up to head straight for coffee. After breakfast, I take off a few warm layers and submit to the intense muscle burn that awaits me on the first uphill of the day. I then find a good hiking pace next to Emily as Kenan and John lead the way and identify our path.

And throughout the day, I continue to open my heart to the small things that awaken my gratitude. I delight in the seemingly endless color variation of the green that covers rock and land. I love the way the clouds lie low in the vast sky above, forming artistic patterns against the steady blue. I appreciate how the silence here has a profound resonance to it, beckoning us each to focus inwardly and listen. And I feel such sweetness for those who are with me on this trail, helping me make this journey a success.

Eventually, we reach the bottom of the caldera wall. The soft, green-moss landscape that has accompanied us for the past few days suddenly gives way to solidified black lava. We lean heavily on our hiking poles as we strain to pull ourselves up the vertical rock face guarding the volcano's core. Small black pebbles present more of a challenge than their innocuous appearance would suggest as I attempt to find my footing on the rocky, sand-like slopes, and I am forced to abandon my normal gait for smaller steps and more intentional foot placements just to stay upright. The hiking is slow going, but the reward waiting for us once we crest the rim is unimaginable until the moment that we glimpse it.

We are hiking into an active volcano.

From the top of the rim, I glance down into a moon-like wonderland. Though I had looked at countless photos of Aniakchak before this trip, no digital image could prepare me for the magic of a landscape born of volcanic activity: lakes the color of gray-tinged teal, thermal rivers in shocking oranges and neon greens. Smaller mountains dot the landscape and beg for exploration, promising unrivaled views of the lava formations that decorate the terrain below.

To get down into the caldera, we utilize a combination of hiking and running, practically skiing into the volcano's depths. It's fun and playful, and as my body picks up speed, I feel the heaviness of the previous days melt away. I have made it to another world. Down in the caldera, we see that the ground is scarred by deep trails. "Grizzly highways," John says as we examine the grooves and accompanying bear footprints. "This is where countless bears have walked for centuries, carving the land with their movement." It feels ancient, and for the rest of the day, my mind returns again and again to images of grizzly tribes claiming this land as their own, leaving behind the paths that become the trails we see today.

I am so relieved when we get to camp and can take off our packs for two entire days that I almost cry.

Exploration inside the caldera is delightful. We climb weird rock faces. We get lost in fields of lava chunks the size of cars. We put our feet in an orange river, which is sadly underwhelming in terms of warmth but is a neat experience nonetheless. We come up with silly names for the small lakes and create songs about them, which we sing when going around blind curves to ward off potential grizzlies. When we tire of our own songs, we come back to our tried-and-true alert anthem: "Hey bear… you're an all-star… get your game on.…"

My happiest times of the trip are the days in the caldera. We find ancient fossils in the rocks along the river. We sleep under starry skies and wake to striking sunrises of blood red and piercing orange. We eat lunch in the rain and then race in the sun along the lava rim. We rejoice in experiencing what few have seen.

Throughout the trip, Kenan shares one of his obsessions with us: stories of alien and fairy abductions of hikers throughout the world. Legends of people who disappeared and were found dead years later, buried under the roots of a huge tree. Someone lost without a trace but later identified in a foreign land not knowing who she was. People who suddenly vanish off trail, as if into thin air, leaving not a trace. Kenan explains that these supernatural attacks often happen in boulder fields, so when we walk through a potentially risky rock-strewn landscape, I always check in to make sure he's still with us.

The second night in the caldera, perhaps thanks to Kenan's stories, I legitimately think I am about to be the victim of an alien abduction.

I wake in the middle of the night to noxious fumes filling my tent. Breathing is almost impossible as my airways close in response to the burning miasma that has displaced the clean Alaskan air. Still half-asleep and having no idea what is happening, I start to panic. Is this a random release of some type of sulfide from the depths of the volcano? Am I having one of those nightmares where you're caught between being asleep and awake and can't tell which world you're in? Or is something supernatural about to happen?

Eventually, the air clears a bit, and my exhaustion wins out over my fear (after several minutes of intense coughing), so I go back to sleep. But before I lie back down, I lick my lips just to see if there's any evidence of my horrifying ordeal. My lips taste of cayenne.

When I make my way down to the food tent in the morning, I weigh my options. Should I tell John that I had possibly experienced an attempted alien abduction? Or should I try to explain that maybe I'd somehow been hit with bear spray (a type of mace to prevent a bear attack), despite being alone in my tent in the middle of the night and not having a bear canister with me? Or should I just drink my coffee and chalk it up to some super-strange dream?

I really want to go with the latter but blurt out, "John, I think I was bear sprayed in my tent last night."

John, with the calm demeanor of someone who's spent a serious amount of time either meditating or consuming copious amounts of marijuana, poses a series of soft-spoken questions.

"Did you have the bear spray in your tent last night?"

"No."

"Do you think anyone else got bear sprayed in their tents last night?"

"No."

"Okay," John replies with a tone that says "I want to believe you but have no idea where to take this from here."

When Emily comes down to breakfast, John asks her if she, too, had been bear sprayed in her tent. She replies that she had not. Kenan is asked the same question, and though he responds in the negative as well, he does say, "I did hear Rachel coughing terribly in the middle of the night. Like something was really wrong. I thought that I should probably check on her, but then I decided to go back to sleep instead."

Feeling at least slightly vindicated by Kenan's comments, I leave to start packing up, and there in the middle of our campsite, where our bear spray had been placed for mutual protection, is a very dead pika, a small mountain-dwelling rodent. Upon closer inspection, I realize that this poor pika had probably been enticed by the peppery smell of our bear-strength mace and somehow found the will and strength to chew through the metal canister, only to be met not with the expected yummy treat but with an early demise. My tent, being the closest to this fatal incident, had likely been downwind of the fiery chemical cloud that went directly through my tent wall and into my lungs.

We hold a small but meaningful funeral for our departed furry friend and then bury him in the Alaskan soil.

To exit the volcano, most people raft out of the caldera on a rapid-filled river favored by grizzlies, but we're hiking the four days back to where we'll meet the small plane that will return us to the comforts of an Anchorage hotel. Since none of us has hiked out of the caldera before, and there's no documentation of anyone taking the southern route out, we are truly on our own. We spend hours poring over maps, trying to identify a route that requires the least amount of bushwhacking or river crossing, but the reality of fighting our way through miles of alder brush is inevitable. It's time to see what we're made of.

Every serious hiker has become lost at one time or another and had to bushwhack to safety. It usually means awkwardly hauling yourself over downed logs and through thick brush, all the while trying to avoid snakes and wasp nests and rogue tree branches that could grab your leg and send you flying face-first toward hard ground.

But no matter how many times you might have found yourself lost off trail, nothing—and I mean *nothing*—can prepare you for bushwhacking through alder in Alaska.

Alder trees are about eight feet tall, have thick branches, and grow in thickets where they entwine with their fellow alder friends. Their roots create wave patterns above the ground, and the thickness of their branches and leaves makes it impossible to see your feet, meaning each step carries a high risk of falling. There is no graceful way to move through alder. Every step is a fight. You have to grab the branches in front of you and use brute strength to pull them apart in order to simply take one step, and then your face and arms are hit hard when you release your grip. Hiking through the alders quickly transforms my skin into an abstract painting of purple, blue, and green bruises, accented by blood-red cuts. Every few steps, my foot catches on a root and I fall, but the alder is so thick that the branches easily support not only the 130 pounds of my body weight but also the extra fifty that I carry on my back.

Adding to this misery is the cow parsnip, a plant that's everywhere along the trail. I have an unfortunate allergic reaction to it, breaking out in hives wherever it comes into contact with my skin. This significantly adds to the overall awfulness of the experience. I've never had to dig so deep to find the will to push through. To help distract myself, I create mental games using alphabet challenges, like naming types of food I can't wait to eat when I'm done with this stupid hike (apple crisps, banana chips, cake…) or boys I've kissed throughout my life (Chris, David, Evan…) or songs by the Beatles ("Lucy in the Sky with Diamonds," "Mean Mister Mustard," "Norwegian Wood"…) until I finally fall into a state of near-total disassociation just to keep moving forward.

As evening approaches, and we think we are done with the alder madness and have only a short time between us and camp, we see one final mountain directly ahead that looks like it will be the worst bushwhacking yet. Having already spent my last reserve of resilience, I simply do not think I can make it. I consider my options, which are none. I can't set up my tent and sleep solo by the river, which is ominously called Plenty Bear Creek. I can't turn around and find an easy trail back to anywhere useful. The only option is through the brush.

I am not sure I've ever hiked before where my legs felt like they were on fire. But in that final push through the trees, all I can feel is burn and the tears streaming down my face. I try to come up with catchy cheerleading commentary for every step. I counter the loud chorus of "You are not strong enough for this" with "I have no choice, and I will succeed." I look down and not ahead so as not to get discouraged by how far I still have to go. And I make it. Somehow, I get to the top of that wretched alder-choked

hill and find at its crest a beautiful flat campground along a pristine river. In that moment, I realize that I truly am stronger than I have ever imagined.

The next day, we arrive back where it all started, eleven long days ago. When we reach the airstrip, we throw down our packs in exuberance, and I collapse on the ground. Waiting for the prop plane, I think about all I went through over the previous eleven days. Awful weather, unrelenting elevation gain, the fear of grizzlies, a bear-spray incident, allergic reactions to foliage, and the worst bushwhacking I hope to ever face in my life. And I feel so damn proud of myself. Waiting for that airplane to take us back to civilization, I realize that Aniakchak did not call me to her for beauty or comfort or amazement. She brought me here to show me who I am and what I am capable of. I know now that I will *never* do a hike like that again, but it forever changed the person I am on trail. And in the end, that realization was worth it all.

LOGISTICS

Aniakchak is the definition of backcountry hiking. There are *no* trails in the park. So unless you are amazing with a map, compass, or GPS system, I highly recommend doing this trip with an outfitter. We went with Alaska alpine Adventures, and they were fantastic. They took care of all the logistics for us once we arrived in Anchorage. I have now done two trips with this group and would recommend them to anyone interested in hiking in Alaska.

Choosing a Route

Hiking in Aniakchak is a "choose your own adventure" type of experience. Since there are no trails, you must decide what you want to see in the park and figure out how to get there.

Getting to the Trailhead

We took a prop plane from Anchorage to King Salmon for the start of this hike.

Length and Difficulty

This hike is a hard one. Not only is it physically challenging to walk through the Alaskan tundra, but the mosquitos, unpredictable weather, soggy ground, and elevation changes require a high degree of fitness (both mental and physical). That being said, if you like a good challenge, then you will love this experience.

Our route was about one hundred miles in total.

Accommodations

Your tent.

Best Time to Hike

Anytime from May to August.

Pro Tips

There were a few creature comforts I was really grateful to have on trail. First, a mosquito head net is a must. I also loved having lightweight sun gloves to protect my hands from these bloodsucking creatures. On this trip, I also learned the importance of having a pair of "sacred socks"—i.e., warm socks (the fuzzy type are my favorite) that *never* leave your tent for any reason. Having dry, warm socks at the end of a hard day of hiking is the most delightful indulgence.

BOOKS

Beyond the Moon Crater Myth: A New History of the Aniakchak Landscape: A Historic Resource Study for Aniakchak National Monument and Preserve by Katherine Johnson Ringsmuth (United States Department of the Interior).

REGIONAL RECIPE

One pleasant aspect of the trail was the abundance of wild salmonberries growing throughout the region. Salmonberries look and taste like raspberries, and finding them was always a sweet pick-me-up during the hike. Since salmonberries are not commercially available, you can use raspberries instead. You will also need seven eight-ounce jars with lids for this recipe.

SALMONBERRY JAM

Servings: Approximately 50

INGREDIENTS

4 cups salmonberries (blackberries or rasp-berries work too, either fresh or frozen)

2 cups white sugar

1 (2 oz) package powdered fruit pectin

DIRECTIONS

1. Make sure the jars are clean (a good scrub in soapy water is a great first step) and do not have any cracks in them.

2. Boil water in a large soup pot and immerse the jars until ready to use.

3. If using fresh berries, crush them thoroughly. If you want a seedless jam, you can use a sieve or cheesecloth to remove the seeds.

4. Place crushed or frozen berries in a large pot.

5. Heat berries over high heat and add sugar until you have a full boil. Make sure to stir constantly so the berries do not burn at the bottom of the pan.

6. Once boiling, quickly stir in pectin and return to a boil for exactly one minute. Make sure you stir consistently the entire time. Remove the pan from the heat at the end of the minute.

7. If there's any foam on top, skim it off with a metal spoon before you ladle the berry mixture into the prepared jars. You want to leave about a quarter inch of space at the top of each jar, and it's a good idea to run a spatula around the inside of the jar to remove any air bubbles.

8. Before you put the lid on, make sure to remove any residue from the rim of the jar. Screw the lids on tightly. It can take 24–48 hours for the jam to solidify, so don't despair if it seems runny at first.

9. If you use the jam within two weeks, no other steps are needed! Just refrigerate and enjoy. If you want to preserve the jam for future use, google how to preserve canned goods.

FRANCE, ITALY, AND SWITZERLAND

Tour du Mont Blanc

August 2017

DIFFICULTY: Strenuous | **LENGTH: 105 miles (169 km)** | **ELEVATION GAIN: 32,000 feet (9,753 m)** | **DURATION: 7–14 days**

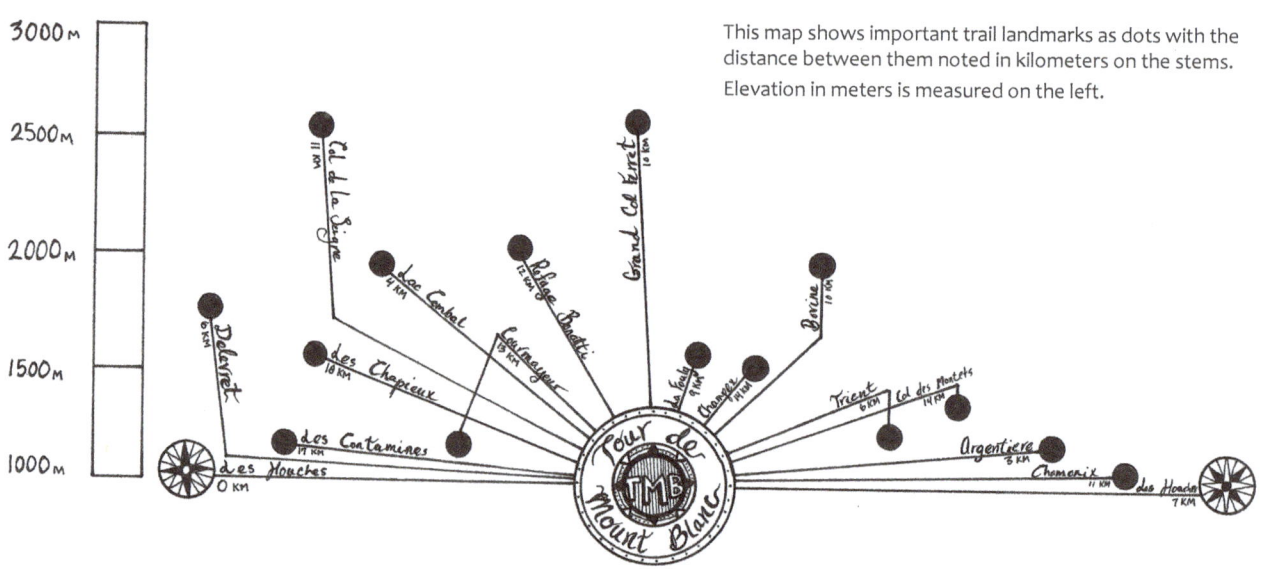

This map shows important trail landmarks as dots with the distance between them noted in kilometers on the stems. Elevation in meters is measured on the left.

Forget not that the earth delights to feel your bare feet and the winds long to play with your hair.

—KAHLIL GIBRAN

●●●● LESSON... Always invite in balance. ●●●●

The streets of Chamonix are lined with rugged outdoor-clothing stores and pastel French patisseries. I stroll down sidewalks surrounded by advertisements for North Face and Patagonia and pass dozens of extremely fit tourists outfitted in the latest hiking gear. They sit in groups of twos and fours and pore over guidebooks while sipping various brands of local beer. I am exploring this cute alpine town after having just left my hotel, which is old and antiquated and verging on musty, if not downright moldy. Walking from the palatial lobby to my shabby room, I felt like the main character in a Wes Anderson film, the hotel the perfect backdrop in a storyline lauding grander days in the French Alps.

The day is perfectly clear, and the deep blue of the sky is interrupted only by the silhouetted mountains, which form a circular wall of massive rock face around the town. As I look at each dominating spire, I try to guess which peak is the famed Mont Blanc (the tallest mountain in western Europe), whose perimeter I will walk for the next ten days. It does not take long to decipher her outline—the mountain has a stately magnificence unrivaled by any of her imposing neighbors. I feel a warm

ember of excitement as I imagine walking her trails, breathing her air, feeling her earth, learning her wisdom.

To fill the hours before dinner, I join other tourists queueing up for a gondola ride that will whisk us onto the famed mountain herself. After just twenty minutes aboard the Aiguille du Midi cable car, the doors open to a noticeably colder mountain path 12,604 feet above sea level. I pull my puffer coat tight and take in the white wonderland of snow-covered granite peaks dotted with distant ice climbers in colorful parkas. Though most of my fellow tourists head directly to the gift shop, I find a secluded red staircase and make my way toward the top viewing platform. Because of the high elevation, I instantly feel those familiar physical symptoms (labored breath and a distended stomach) as I climb the final few stairs to find my way outside.

As I exit the stairwell, I am immediately overwhelmed by the sheer massiveness of the alps and the sea of seemingly endless peaks juxtaposed against the blue-jay hue of the high-altitude sky. I scan the horizon to see if I can identify the mountain trail that will take me 105 miles through three countries. A journey where I'll ascend a total of 32,000 feet, earning the bragging rights of gaining more elevation in ten days than it would take to scale the entire height of Mount Everest. But alas, the trail is too small to spot against the grandeur of the mountain, so I just relax and enjoy the view.

Morning comes quickly after a decent night's sleep, and as I perform a final gear check and braid my hair into my signature pigtails, I notice that my heart rate is elevated. I am nervous about the unknowns that lie ahead, especially because the trail's reputation is that it is not for the faint of heart. I take deep breaths to regulate myself, find some semblance of centeredness, and walk outside to catch the local bus. It is just a short ride to the gondola station at the trek's threshold.

There's a handful of other TMB (Tour du Mont Blanc) hikers that exit the bus with me, and in what could be almost synchronized choreography, we all pull out guide maps and trail notes and check the gondola stops against our hiking itineraries. About twelve of us crowd together at the ticket counter, gazing up at the descending gondola that will soon ferry us skyward. We board as a group, and ascend.

Once the cable car reaches our destination, we step into a flower-filled meadow. I look around to find the trailhead emblazoned with the black and green TMB logo that will serve as my guide for the entirety of my walk. The other hikers are taking their time to readjust their packs and have a last-minute snack, but I feel that familiar urgency I experience at the start of every trail, so I begin to walk. The trail is steep and steady and without switchbacks, and I am quickly winded, cursing the heaviness of my pack (why I followed the packing list recommended by the travel agency instead of trusting my own intuition is completely lost on me at this moment). But eventually, the intense exertion subsides, and I find my rhythm and cadence along the trail.

The TMB is hands down the most beautiful hike I have ever experienced. The alpine wonderland of craggy peaks, flower-filled meadows, endless vistas, and postcard-worthy backdrops creates a consistent state of amazement. Each day includes thousands of feet of ascension and descension with truly jaw-dropping views at the top of every mountain pass (of which there is at least one daily, if not several).

Though the demands of hiking these trails is unrelenting, the scenery is more than reward enough for the physical intensity. As an added delight, the trail is filled with adventurers from all over the world. We congregate at night in communal mountain huts to share food and stories about our homes, our travels, and the reasons we keep coming back to the mountains.

As I make my way through the three countries that the TMB traverses, I notice that the sleeping huts embody the distinct culture of their particular homeland. In France, it's a signal that the meal is ending when an antique music box is wheeled into the dining room. With the turn of a handle, the room fills with song, and the French hikers sing together to pay nostalgic tribute to the melodies of their country. I smile both at their enthusiasm and in sweet recognition of how music can become a thread that stitches together the lives of strangers on trail.

To me, Switzerland's huts feel the most subdued of the three countries' accommodations. They are decorated in simple mountain memorabilia and have an atmosphere of quiet reverence. Not surprisingly, the Swiss huts serve the best chocolate.

And then there is Italy.

In addition to TMB hikers, the Italian huts are filled with both day hikers who've braved the trails up the mountain and tourists who have simply opted for a gondola ride to sit amidst the extraordinary views and eat plates of pasta and cheese. I've spent the entire day pushing through a particularly challenging uphill stretch over Mont de la Saxe, which was listed in my guidebook as an alternative to the more heavily trafficked main trail. Taking this off-

the-beaten-path route means I spent my daylight hours in glorious and delicious silence. Understandably, it's a bit jarring when I arrive at the crowded hut and have to quickly transition from my peaceful mountain solitude to alpine party time.

The energy in the Italian huts is beyond boisterous. As I enter the main hall, I'm greeted with the smell of cigarettes, the sounds of laughter, and the continual clinking of beer steins. People are joyously honoring another completed day on trail (or perhaps simply being in such an incredible locale), and I feel almost guilty claiming a table just for myself amidst the groups of friends congregating in raucous clusters. But it is far past my normal lunchtime, and the allure of a big plate of pasta quickly trumps my fear of being seen as an awkward loner in a celebratory environment.

But I am not alone the entire time—when dinner comes a few hours later, I am assigned to a table with a Canadian couple and two Frenchmen. One of the latter is a doctor, and the other an alternative healer like myself. My rudimentary French and the healer's broken English do not do much to create conversational flow, but I find something about him enthralling. I love his sweet manner and the way he looks into my eyes with such openness and sincerity when we try to converse. I go to sleep thinking about the soft contours of his face, the copper glint of his hair, and the melody of his voice as he reached for words in English to try to form a connection.

In the morning, we find each other again, and over oatmeal and coffee, he tries to explain how important essential oils are in his self-care routine. When words we have in common become too hard to find, he simply takes out a vial of mint oil from his bag and tenderly places a few drops on my forehead and temples.

I smell its soothing scent for days.

The last day of my TMB adventure is filled with mixed emotions. My body is tired, but my soul feels elevated. As the number of miles ahead begins to dwindle, I work to commit every last detail of my surroundings to memory. The way the trail tightly hugs the undulating mountainside. The medley of summer flowers that paints the landscape in purples and pinks and yellows. The tintinnabulation of the bells worn by cattle in nearby fields. The softness of the ground beneath my feet and the warmth of the sun as it illuminates the alpine landscape. There is a truly spacious sacredness to this land.

When I see the cable car in the distance that signifies the completion of my hike, I race toward it to feel one final push of physical exertion before this adventure reaches its end. I am winded as I enter the compartment but also happy, smelly, and deeply content. From the window, I watch the mountains in appreciation as they fade from view during our descent.

As I gently float toward the town, I reflect upon my time in these mountains and feel deep gratitude for the unprecedented beauty I have seen. I have pushed myself past physical limits time and time again on the TMB, and am so deeply proud of all that I have accomplished on trail. This journey has been epic, but the time for deep reflection is now complete. As soon as the cable car arrives in Chamonix, my thoughts quickly turn to what is now singing to my heart: a celebratory beer, a well-earned plate of french fries, and getting my next commemorative dot tattoo.

LOGISTICS

The traditional TMB route starts in Les Houches, a ten-minute bus ride from Chamonix. Most hikers choose to hike counterclockwise so as to leave the part from Col de la Forclaz to Argentière for the end, which is often regarded as the route's grand finale. But truly, you'll be guaranteed unbelievable beauty every day on this hike, regardless of where you begin or which direction you take.

Choosing a Route

The TMB is well marked, and there is a standard route that people take through the three countries. However, most stretches have alternative trail options outlined in the Kev Reynolds book listed below.

Getting to the Trailhead

The town of Chamonix is easily reached by shuttle from the Geneva airport, which is an hour and a half away. From Chamonix, the Line 1 bus will connect you to Les Houches, where the Bellevue cable car will take you to the beginning of the trail.

Length and Difficulty

The TMB is a seriously challenging hike. You will summit at least one mountain pass daily and will sometimes face more than 5,000 feet of climbing in a single day.

This hike can be completed in as little as seven days or as many as fourteen, depending on the level of intensity you desire.

Accommodations

It's possible to tent camp along the entire trail. However, most people choose to stay in either the mountain huts or simple village hotels. The advantage of staying in the huts is getting to meet people from around the world.

Best Time to Hike

The best time to hike the TMB is from mid-June through early September.

Pro Tips

I hired the guide group Distant Journeys to coordinate the logistics of my hike. This way, all my reservations and transfers were arranged in advance. Many hikers I met paid to have their luggage transferred to their accommodations so they could carry lighter packs. I didn't choose this option but wished I had—hiking would have been more enjoyable if I had been carrying less weight.

I recommend bringing some light synthetic rope and clothespins, along with a small bottle of Dr. Bronner's Pure-Castile Liquid Soap, to do laundry in the mountain huts.

BOOKS

The Tour of Mont Blanc: Complete Two-Way Trekking Guide by Kev Reynolds (Cicerone Trekking Guides).

LOCAL LANGUAGES

German

Thank you: Vielen dank (FEEL-in dah-nk)
Please: Bitte (BIT-ah)
I'm sorry: Es tut mir leid (Es TOOT me-er light)

French

Thank you: Merci beaucoup (MER-sea BO-ku)
Please: S'il vous plaît (Seal VOO play)
I'm sorry: Je suis désolé (Je sue-ee DAY-so-lay)

Italian

Thank you: Grazie (GRAH-tsee)
Please: Per favore (PAYR fah-for-AY)
I'm sorry: Mi dispiace (Me dis-PEE-AH-chay)

Nothing tastes better at the end of a long hike than a big bowl of pasta. This recipe reminds me of eating at a lively Italian hut after a tough day on trail.

ARTICHOKE GARLIC PASTA

Serves 4–6

INGREDIENTS

rotini pasta (enough for 4–6 people)

1 small yellow onion, chopped

1 tbsp olive oil

1 (16 oz) jar marinated artichoke hearts

4–6 garlic cloves, minced

1 tsp lemon juice

1 cup marinara sauce

4–6 sun-dried tomatoes, chopped

1 tsp oregano

2 tsp dried basil

salt and pepper to taste

DIRECTIONS

1. Cook pasta according to package instructions.

2. While pasta is cooking, sauté onions in olive oil in a medium saucepan over medium-high heat until the onions are translucent.

3. Add artichokes, garlic, and lemon juice. Cook for another 5 minutes until the sauce has reduced.

4. Scoop out a quarter cup of pasta water and add to the saucepan, along with marinara sauce, sun-dried tomatoes, oregano, basil, salt, and pepper.

5. Cook for about 2 minutes, until tomatoes are warmed through.

6. Drain pasta and toss with sauce.

The Overland Track

November 2017

DIFFICULTY: Moderate | **LENGTH: 40 miles (64 km)** | **ELEVATION GAIN: 4,793 feet (1,461 m)** | **DURATION: 4–10 days**

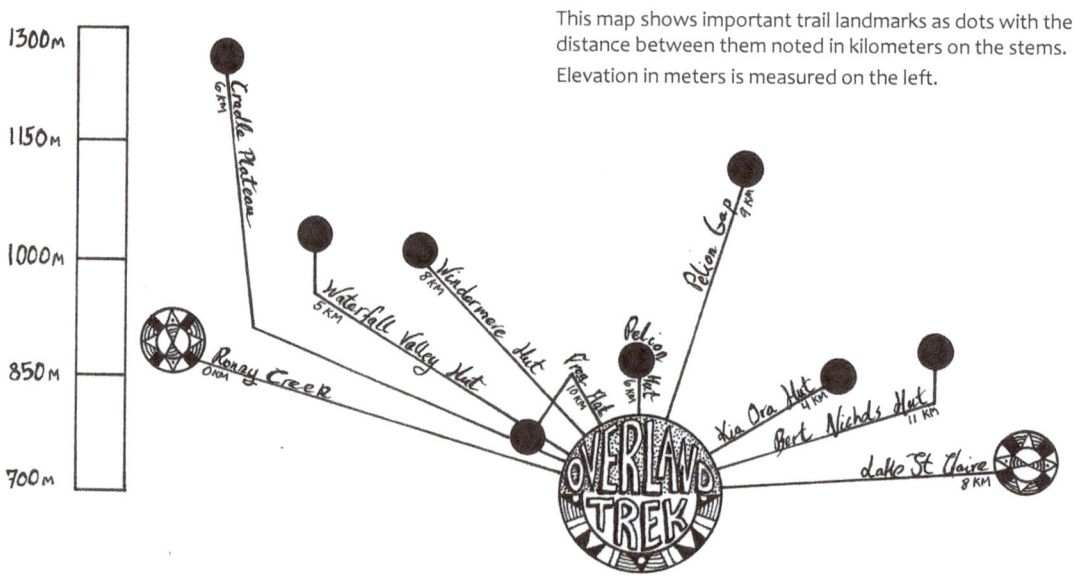

This map shows important trail landmarks as dots with the distance between them noted in kilometers on the stems. Elevation in meters is measured on the left.

*And suddenly you know:
it's time to start something new and
trust the magic of beginnings.*

—MEISTER ECKHART

●●●●● LESSON... Ask for help. ●●●●●

While riding the bus to the trailhead for the Overland Track, our group is asked to share our previous personal hiking experience. Immediately after I finish, I realize my introduction probably sounded way more boastful than intended, and I instantly wish for a do-over. I am the only American on a bus full of Australians, so there's probably already a major mark against me. I realize I should have been more subtle in how I talked about the places I've hiked and the experiences I've had. The chilly reaction from the others is a reminder that I really need to find a better way to talk about my trekking experiences without sounding like an over-the-top ad for *National Geographic*.

Lesson learned.

The group is a mix of a few couples around my age and some older men who seem like they've been around the trekking block a time or two. Their skin has that rugged, leathery look of people who've enjoyed many days of adventuring in the open air. Our college-aged guides exude seemingly unlimited enthusiasm, and we spend our first hours on trail listening to them share everything from their favorite breakfast foods to their nascent aspirations, sprinkled with some details about the

upcoming trail challenges. The most daunting of these is the "opportunity" to become one of the few people who can say they've completed the 007, which involves jumping in two freezing lakes (thus the 0 for 0 degrees) and ascending one serious mountain summit (at more than 700 meters—thus the 7—or approximately 2,300 feet). The prize for joining the 007? Serious bragging rights.

Group trips have always been hard for me. The second my feet touch the trail, I feel a deep longing to be left on my own. Being obligated to make small talk day in, day out feels like proverbial nails on the chalkboard of my soul. I came to Tasmania to gain insight from my time hiking, not to make new friends. I want to experience one of the most beautiful trails in the world, the Overland Track, which entails six days walking through Cradle Mountain-Lake St. Clair National Park. To traverse a landscape where boardwalks are as plentiful as dirt trails. Where trees and foliage create unfamiliar shapes against clear sky. Where kangaroos and wombats roam freely. Where even the stars in the night sky create constellations unknown to me.

So why did I choose to do this hike with a group instead of going solo? Well, I grew up believing that Australia was filled with an inordinate number of reptiles, invertebrates, and other animals that would kill me given half a chance. Any crawling or climbing creature could be a potential fast track to the "other side." And though I consider myself fairly capable at navigating around bears, rattlesnakes, storms, and freezing weather conditions, I had no experience in challenges of the venomous variety. I figured if I suffered a potentially lethal bite, it would work to my benefit to be surrounded by those trained to deal with such things.

Adding to the allure of the group option was that the company I'd chosen, Tasmanian Expeditions (TE), has exclusive access to the only truly nice huts on the trail. Although communal huts are available for people hiking on their own, staying in the TE huts includes clean sheets, local wines, and food so expertly prepared, you'd never know it came from a can or a bag. The huts are so thoughtfully curated that they even contain copies of the same books so you can read a chapter in one hut and pick up where you left off when you make it to the next.

I considered my discomfort with group dynamics a small price to pay for increased survival odds and a bit of pampering.

The first stretch of the Overland Track is the most alpine in its beauty. The peaks of Cradle Mountain juxtapose starkly against the tranquil lake below, which makes me feel as if I am hiking in Europe and not the Land Down Under. I feel energized by my surroundings, and my feet gain speed as I search for solitude, trying to put as much distance as possible between me and the other hikers in my group, without inviting a reprimand from our young guides. Happily, I seem to be getting away with my isolationist strategy. Soon their laughter and instant-friend chatter sound far behind me, until eventually, I'm aware of only the mountains around me, the sound of my breath, the feel of my footsteps, and the beauty of it all.

And then I trip and fall.

I stretch both hands out in front of me to brace against the impending impact, and as my palms hit the rough-pebbled ground, my right wrist snaps in an unnatural angle. Pain shoots up my arm, and I crumble onto the trail.

For a few moments, everything goes black.

When I eventually return to my body, my vision is slightly blurred and my breath labored. I try to move my hand and gratefully find that my fingers shift ever so slightly, which I hope is a sign that nothing is broken. But the pain I feel is unusually intense for a sprain, and before long, I resign myself to the fact that after just a few short hours of hiking, my trip is most likely over. Worse, I might need to be airlifted off the mountain. I am heartbroken, embarrassed, and dreading the moment the group finds me like this.

Oddly, despite this being the most popular trail in Tasmania, only a few people walk past while I wait. Some offer to help, while others seem so uncomfortable with the sight of a person half-passed out in the bushes, they simply step over me. It takes about forty-five minutes for my group to finally arrive, and I can sense their shock when they round the corner to find me semiconscious. The irony that hours earlier I was regaling them with stories of the many foreign peaks I'd bagged feels humiliating, for now I'm reduced to needing rescue because of one small misstep.

As luck would have it, our group includes two quirky and kind doctors named Andy and Julian. And even though their expertise is respectively sleep and the lower GI tract, they have enough knowledge to help with my yet-to-be-diagnosed injury. Together we determine that I should try to walk the half-mile to our hut for the evening. The plan is to pump me full of some serious anti-inflammatories, feed me a few good meals, and then, in the morning, reassess my ability to continue the trek. If moving on is not possible for me, we'll come up with an evacuation strategy, which will either mean hiking me out or paying for a helicopter lift to the nearest emergency room. They hastily create a makeshift sling for my arm, and somehow I find the strength to walk.

Depending on the help of my group is instantly a challenge. Under most circumstances, I'm a fiercely independent person. I learned this survival strategy growing up in a family where love and kindness were sometimes a limited resource. Living in a home lacking in warmth, I coped by rebelling. By the time I turned fourteen, my parents had had enough of my challenging ways, and off to reform school I went.

Being sent away so young teaches you to fend for yourself, and I quickly learned how to survive in what was at times a ruthless environment in school. As a young teenager, I got a crash course in how to take care of myself, which helped me rise above things like a counselor's emotional abuse, a fellow student's projected rage, and being forced to survive solo in the mountains for four days during a mandatory outdoor experience. My rough-and-tumble adolescence taught me that the only person whom I could truly depend on was myself. Reliance on others, I learned, led only to disappointment, struggle, and abandonment.

And yet this first night on the Overland Track—and for the entirety of the trip—I have to learn to ask for help. I can't use my right hand or arm at all. I can't even take off my boots. I can't pull my hair into a ponytail, and I can't apply sunscreen to my face. Everything that necessitates two hands is out of reach for me. And just like that, thanks to my fall, a group of sixteen strangers becomes my only hope to complete the trip.

The timing of this injury and its lessons are not lost on me. Before I left for Australia, I had met someone back home. And not the type of someone where I knew the partnership would have an imminent expiration date but someone with whom I could sense the distinct possibility of sharing a life. For me, Matt embodied compassion and thoughtfulness, and I knew right away that he'd done his emotional work. He was forthcoming and demonstrative and showed up for me in ways that no partner had before.

Independence and self-reliance will always be a cornerstone of who I am, and yet I fully knew that any sustainable partnership would require a willingness to step into vulnerability. After I fell, I sensed that once I returned home, this injury was going to be an invitation to let someone who was already occupying space in my heart take care of me in the physical sense as well. This was terrifying to me, yet inevitable. It was going to be the only way I could step into the "us" of love.

Fortunately, my group could not be kinder. They smear my toast with Vegemite. They pour me glasses of wine. They gently place the shoulder strap of my bag over my arm. And they offer warm words of encouragement when I'm grimacing in pain. Within days, this group of "others" quickly becomes a fiercely protective family, and as hard as it is for me, I let them.

Strangers on the trail are less kind. Several nasty comments are thrown at me, implying or stating directly that my choice to complete the hike while injured endangers my entire group. I walk past picnicking hikers who call me "irresponsible" and "selfish," and at least once, I duck behind a bush to let myself have a good cry, especially after a particularly hateful woman berates me in front of a large group of trekkers. It is unfathomable to me why so many feel the need to be so judgmental, but each time I'm left in tatters by cruel comments, my trail family is right there to literally and figuratively pick me up and help me find myself once again.

Being in pain on trail makes me that much more grateful for the beauty of my surroundings. Having come so close to losing the opportunity to hike the Overland Track makes each tree, each lagoon, each plant feel precious. I even grow to appreciate hiking with others and learning from their life journeys, enjoying the experience of our co-created adventure.

The day before our trip is set to end, we find ourselves at the edge of a wooded glen. Where the trail enters the forest, the tree branches form an enveloping green canopy, sweetly mingling with one another in the cool breeze. There's a wooden boardwalk marking the path between where we stand and a flower-filled meadow on the other side of the trees. Before we enter, our guides invite us to walk in silence, one at a time, through the foliage. I watch as the others start shifting from communal experience to individual reflection, and I enjoy the joyous unfolding in their facial expressions as they begin their individual walks. When my turn comes, I set a mindful intention: to be aware of the shapes of the leaves above me, to notice the intricately textured patterns carved in the brown-bark trunks, and to bring my gaze toward the upwardly rising branches. This forest… this moment… this journey. I silently connect to everything around and within.

My last night on the Overland Track, I choose bravery over fear and set up my sleeping bag on a wooden platform under the stars, alongside the tour staff members. Earlier that day, we'd come across the second-most-poisonous snake in Australia; it slithered its way across our path, paying no mind to our presence. Images of this tiger snake, as well as scorpions and tarantulas, fill my head as I position my sleeping bag in this vulnerable spot outside, and I hope I have enough karmic points to survive the night. But as I witness the never-ending expanse of stars fill the night sky, and the Southern Cross begins to shine brightly against the velvety darkness, my fears transform into deep gratitude. As I take in that vast celestial wonderland, I know this experience has expanded me perhaps more than any other. Being thrown into vulnerability and pain and ultimately making it through thanks only to the help from near strangers has permanently shifted something inside of me. I know that because of Tasmania, I'm now ready to go home and venture into the most unfamiliar territory of all: love.

LOGISTICS

From October to May (encompassing Australian spring, summer, and fall), a permit is necessary to book the trek, and only fifty are available each day. To find out more about how to secure a permit and other trek requirements, visit the section about permits on the website for Tasmanian Expeditions.

Bookings for the Overland Track do fill up, so if you're interested in hiking it during the temperate months and especially during the summer season, try to make your reservation at least a month or two in advance.

If you choose to go with Tasmanian Expeditions, they take care of all permits and provide their own huts and food. Another advantage is that their guides are amazing and provide in-depth education about the land, the history, and the culture of Tasmania.

Choosing a Route

There is one main route that makes up the official trek. However, there are additional side trips that can be added to extend your time on trail.

Getting to the Trailhead

There are a couple of ways to get to the beginning of this trek. First, you can fly to Sydney and then catch a regional flight to Launceston, where you can arrange ground transportation to the trailhead. Alternatively, you can take a ferry from Melbourne to Devonport in Tasmania.

If you're hiking during Australia's summer months, you'll need to start the Overland Track at Ronny Creek in Cradle Mountain-Lake St. Clair National Park. In winter, you can start from either direction. The closest major cities to Cradle Mountain are Devonport and Launceston.

Because the trek starts in the north at the Cradle Mountain visitor center and finishes in the south at the Lake St. Clair visitor center, you'll need to figure out the logistics of starting and finishing in two separate locations (such as booking a shuttle in advance).

Length and Difficulty

Most people complete the hike in six days, though it can be done in as few as four and in as many as ten. The hike is considered moderate in terms of exertion and fitness level.

Accommodations

All public huts and campgrounds on the Overland Track are first come, first served and open to all self-guided walkers, and you can't reserve a camping platform or bunk in a hut ahead of time. Therefore, if you're doing a self-guided hike, it's a good idea to bring camping gear in case the huts are full. However, anyone is allowed to cook in the huts, no matter where they're sleeping.

Best Time to Hike

The Overland Track is most commonly hiked in the Australian summer, from December to March. However, each season offers unique advantages for experiencing the trail. To read more about the Overland Track throughout the seasons, check out the blog on Tasmanian Expeditions' website.

Pro Tips

It can be very wet on this trail, so be sure to bring really good rain gear and water-resistant shoes. Also, there's nowhere to get food after you start, so bring in all your favorite snacks to enjoy.

If you have time to spend in Tasmania after your hike, make it a priority to visit the Museum of Old and New Art in Hobart. If incredible and immersive artistic experiences sing to you, this museum will absolutely amaze.

Finally, if you're a woman, never refer to your "map of Tasmania." I learned about this slang term in a most embarrassing way (I'll leave you to google it).

BOOKS

Hiking the Overland Track: Tasmania: Cradle Mountain-Lake St. Clair National Park by
    Warwick Sprawson (Cicerone Press Limited).

My fellow hikers who hail from Australia were shocked at how deeply I fell in love with Vegemite. Just thinking about Vegemite makes my stomach feel all warm and happy inside. Here is a healthy version you can make at home.

HOMEMADE VEGEMITE
Servings: 10-12

INGREDIENTS
- ½ cup black tahini paste/spread
- ¼ cup coconut aminos
- 3 tbsp nutritional yeast flakes
- 2 tsp coconut oil
- 2 tsp apple cider vinegar
- 1 soft Medjool date, pitted
- 2 tbsp lemon juice
- 2 tbsp miso
- 1 tsp cinnamon
- ¼ tsp smoked paprika
- ½ tsp sea salt (or more if you'd like!)

DIRECTIONS
1. In a food processor, combine all ingredients. Process for 10 seconds.
2. Remove the blade and scrape down the bowl. Continue blending for another 8–10 seconds until the paste is smooth.
3. Spread on toast or crackers and enjoy! If not using all of the recipe immediately, store in a sterilized glass jar or container in the refrigerator.

Dana Nature Reserve to Petra

December 2017

DIFFICULTY: Moderate | LENGTH: **58 miles (93 km)** | ELEVATION GAIN: **7,000 feet (2,133 m)** | DURATION: **5 days**

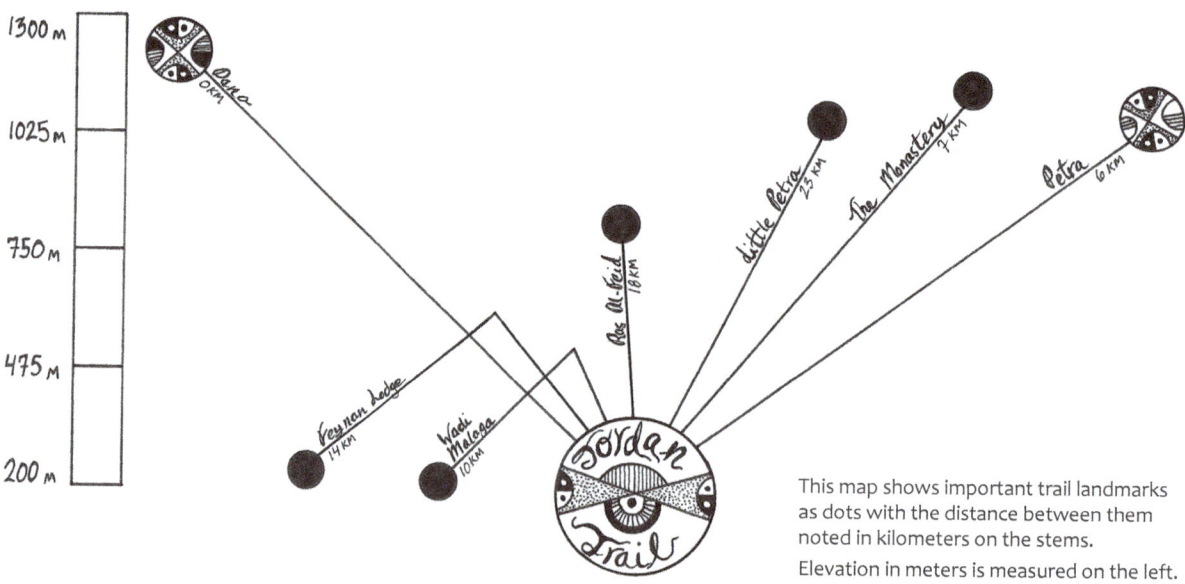

This map shows important trail landmarks as dots with the distance between them noted in kilometers on the stems.

Elevation in meters is measured on the left.

The earth has its music for those who will listen.

—REGINALD VINCENT HOLMES

●●●● LESSON... Treasure the stillness. ●●●●

A solitary bird flies through this valley cut of stone and sand. Alone, I watch as it navigates subtle wind patterns to find its way toward where it will make its home for the night. The other hikers in my group go ahead of me to explore an interesting geological formation in the canyon, but I pause here, stopped short by an unfamiliar sensation. Silence. Not quiet per se but a degree of silence that I have perhaps never experienced. It feels like the very essence of the absence of sound. There is a vastness to it—so much so that it renders me almost paralyzed as I sit within it on the valley floor, attempting to absorb the enormity and simplicity of this moment.

Saying that desert landscapes are "otherworldly" feels like a cliché. And yet, any other descriptor seems insufficient to depict this place and the energy it radiates. Words such as "vast," "epic," and "mysterious" capture pieces of what it's like to be within this realm, but attempting to sum up its magic in words feels futile. So instead, I simply let myself *feel* into being fully here in the Jordanian desert, within these canyon walls.

There's a quality to complete silence that is almost as bone-chilling as the winter wind in my hometown of Chicago. The silence penetrates past skin and even organs to find its way into the core of our being. I want the desert to know how deeply I appreciate the gift of this moment, of being a piece of the musical orchestration of its silent layers. The absence of any aural stimulus invites in a deeper sense of mindfulness, and with sharpened eyes, I take in the subtle rock formations around me, noticing the sapling-size trees fighting their way through stone and sand. And I invite myself to just be.

I begin this five-day hike on a cloudy, sprinkling day in the Dana Biosphere Nature Reserve. The scenery at the start is pretty but underwhelming. As always, when not struck with an immediate "wow" factor, I attempt to find beauty in the small things I pass—species of trees and flowers new to me, the interesting variation in the rock formations, the muted greens and yellows that dot the trail's trajectory. But it's not until day three, when the desert displays vast mountainous silhouettes against its pink and yellow stone backdrop, that I understand its greatness.

The desert here is a trickster. From a distance, it makes you think there is uniformity to its geography. But this is not the case—it's a mere mirage. The desert in the western part of Jordan is as varied as any alpine landscape. With its unearthly towers and the sandy paths of its vertical climbs, the desert holds a beauty that is stunning in its lack of predictability.

Our group of travelers comes from around the world, and we spend Christmas night together on trail drinking wine under a starry sky while sharing family stories from our varied traditions. At the end of evening, we fall asleep to the sacred sounds of the Qur'an being chanted by the staff members who are making this journey possible for us. The next evening, after a massive sandstorm fills the air with the roar of uncontrollable wind and destroys our campsite, we work as a unified team to evacuate to

the safety of the nearest town before returning to the trail the next day. By the fifth day, the trail is filled with the sounds of laughter and chatty camaraderie. Though our backgrounds vastly differ, we're bound together through our mutual kindness, openness to adventure, and love of the earth.

On our last day, we wake early and begin a solemn hike to a summit through a final mountain pass. Perhaps because our journey's end is near, I find the scenery on this part of the trail the most beautiful. The mountains present themselves in all their grandeur as we push through this final challenge to the summit. When we reach that extraordinary viewpoint, we finally see the reason we've all come here—the ancient city of Petra. This famous, massive archeological site dating to around 300 BCE is considered one of the wonders of the world. We spend the next several hours exploring its pink structures and stunningly well-preserved ruins. And though our journey here was only five days long, each of us walks into this ancient city slightly changed. This desert now feels like a part of our hearts, and the history of this land forms a piece of the woven fabric of our memories.

At the trip's end, I give a goodbye hug to our cook, and he hands me a CD. When I look down, I see that it's an audio recording of the Qur'an, the words of which have served as my lullaby each night and as my waking melody each morning. He looks into my eyes and tells me not to listen to it with my ears but to hear it with my heart. I hold this precious gift in my hands as I etch this moment into my memory, taking one more look at the vast desert that has held me for this journey. With profound gratitude, I board the van to return home.

LOGISTICS

The hike from the Dana Nature Reserve to Petra is part of the Jordan Trail, which opened in 2017. The long-distance hike stretches the length of Jordan from Umm Qais in the north to Aqaba in the south. The Dana-to-Petra section can be hiked solo or with a group. If you're interested in solo hiking, visit the official trail website for information on transportation, campsites, and permits.

I joined a group expedition through KE Adventures, and I'm really glad that I did. They provided everything from transportation, route selection, and tents to the most amazing food. For information about this trip, visit their site.

Choosing a Route

Route selection in the desert can be a bit tricky. However, the Jordan Trail website has information on the best way to reach Petra from Dana. In all honesty, I was very glad to be walking with a group since trail markers are few and far between.

Getting to the Trailhead

Amman is the closest city to Dana with an international airport, and it's easy to arrange transport from Amman to Dana. You'll have to book a shuttle to return to Amman from Petra since this is a point-to-point hike.

Length and Difficulty

This hike takes four to five days and covers fifty-two miles. Though the trail is not overly challenging, there is one stretch with more than 2,500 feet of elevation gain in one day.

Accommodations

This hike consists exclusively of camping in the desert.

Best Time to Hike

It's best to do this hike when it's not summer because of the extreme heat. Anytime from January to April or from October to December is ideal.

Pro Tips

I highly recommend having lightweight gaiters to cover the tops of your shoes to prevent sand from finding its way into your footwear. I adore the options at Dirty Girl Gaiters and never go on a hiking trip without them. Also, because there are stinging scorpions in the desert, be sure to check your shoes and clothes before you put them on to ensure there are no unwanted visitors hiding within.

BOOKS

Hiking in Jordan: Trails In and Around Petra, Wadi Rum and the Dead Sea Area by Dr. Gregory F. Maassen, Chris Grant, and Martin Smit (CreateSpace Independent Publishing Platform).

LOCAL LANGUAGE: ARABIC

Thank you: شكراً (SHUH-kran)

Please: من فضلك (min FUD-luck)

I'm sorry: إني آسفة (inee AH-sifa) if you are a woman speaking

I'm sorry: إني آسف (inee AH-sif) if you are a man speaking

REGIONAL RECIPE

Every night on trail, we enjoyed a feast! And every dish was more delicious than the last. However, if I had to pick a favorite, it would absolutely be the *ful mudammas*, a stew of cooked fava beans served with olive oil and cumin.

FUL MUDAMMAS

Serves 6–8

a

INGREDIENTS

3 garlic cloves

1 tsp whole cumin seeds

Salt

2 (15 oz) cans fava beans (California Garden is great brand)

3 tbsp tahini

2–3 tbsp lemon juice (adjust more or less to taste)

1 tbsp apple cider vinegar

⅛ cup olive oil (plus extra for serving)

pitas

DIRECTIONS

1. Toast cumin seeds in a skillet on high heat, consistently shaking the pan for 1–2 minutes. Be careful as they can burn easily.

2. Place garlic cloves, toasted cumin seeds, and a pinch of salt in a mortar and pestle and crush until seeds are cracked and garlic is the consistency of a chunky paste.

3. Pour two cans of fava beans and the liquid of one can into a medium saucepan and combine with tahini and garlic paste. Cook over medium-high heat, stirring frequently, until liquid turns thick and sauce-like, about 5 minutes.

4. Add lemon juice, apple cider vinegar, olive oil, and salt to taste.

5. Transfer everything into a ceramic or glass bowl and mash with a potato masher until there is a chunky consistency. Serve with warm toasted pita and a drizzle of olive oil on top.

Torres del Paine

February 2018

DIFFICULTY: Moderate | LENGTH: 85 miles (137 km) | ELEVATION GAIN: 13,290 feet (4,051 m) | DURATION: 5–10 days

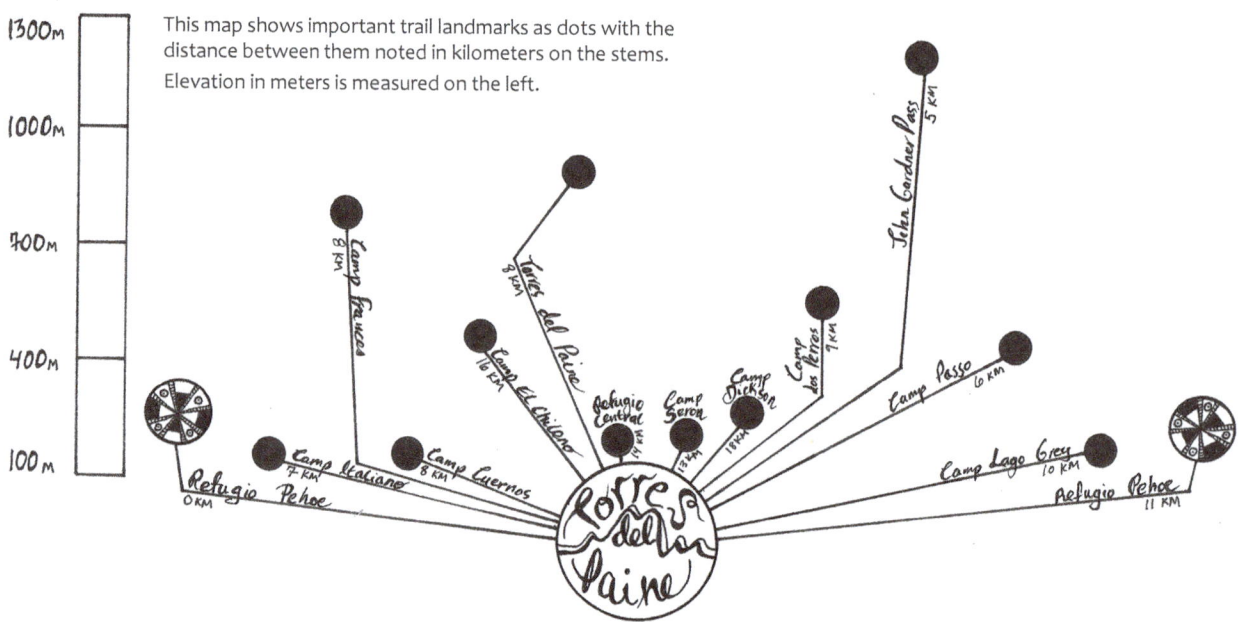

This map shows important trail landmarks as dots with the distance between them noted in kilometers on the stems. Elevation in meters is measured on the left.

You need special shoes for hiking—
and a bit of a special soul as well.

—TERRI GUILLEMETS

LESSON... Trust the unfolding.

It takes three full days of travel, but I have finally reached the park entrance of the Torres del Paine. After watching the safety-information video, I sign the obligatory papers promising not to light fires, leave litter, or cause harm to this Chilean national park. However, though I'm a dedicated rule follower, I'm struggling to accept the "do not hike alone early in the morning" guidance. I know the pumas here typically hunt for prey around dawn, and though being attacked by a puma is not high on my tourist wish list, the idea of hiking among the mob of park visitors (who tend to start late morning) is even less appealing than a potential encounter with a carnivorous feline. I decide I'll take my chances once on trail.

After the signing of papers is complete, I locate the boat shuttle, about a mile from the park entrance, that will take me to the trailhead. There's a flurry of commotion at the dock as people compete to throw their backpacks into a big pile on the boat. For some reason, they seem anxious to claim a seat on one of the wooden benches, even though the next shuttle will arrive in only thirty minutes. I stand back, choosing not to enter the fray, and am one of the final passengers to board. As I make my way towards the front of the boat, I chuckle silently at how clean and fresh we look and smell and imagine what we'll be like on the return ride nine days from now. The boat gains speed, and I feel the slightest spray of water from our wake as we begin the journey across the small Lago Pehoe to the start of the trail.

To my right, a few benches away, sits a blonde woman about my age; we seem to be the only women hikers not connected to another person or group. I try not to stare at her, but I'm laughing to myself as I take a quick inventory of her clothing, which bears an uncanny resemblance to mine. The same Salomon hiking boots. The same brand of gray pants. And a long-sleeved, light-fleece layer—in the same shade of teal—to keep warm against the chilly mountain mornings. Aside from the differences in our packs, it looks like we went on a communal REI outfitting trip to find our shared signature look.

I introduce myself immediately .

Sarah is a nurse from Idaho whose passion for hiking the world's most beautiful trails rivals my own. She has had the privilege of trekking some of the earth's most splendid terrain, and I delight in knowing that I'll have nine full days to hear her hiking stories and find inspiration from her journeys.

We compare our Chilean itineraries and realize that, aside from one night, we're staying in the same huts and campsites during our entire time here. We agree to dine together every evening during our trip, and I am so relieved that awkward mealtime seating configurations with strangers will not be part of my story for this hike. When the boat lands, we exchange goodbyes for now and start off separately on the trail.

Patagonia is an ever-changing combination of lush and harsh. The trails avoid the relative ease of switchbacks, opting instead for straight vertical climbs up and down rocky mountain pathways and passes where stunning spring flowers decorate the craggy mountainside. In terms of views, our intense physical effort traversing undulating mountains is rewarded every few miles with the panorama of an alpine lake shimmering with the sun's reflection and surrounded by glaciers.

This trail is more popular than I'd prefer, but I find if I leave the mountain huts by 5:30 a.m. (braving potential puma encounters), I can savor a few glorious hours of quiet solitude. The first few days are pleasant yet uneventful. I enjoy the varied scenery and the novelty of hiking in South America, but I feel a deep longing to connect with where I am and what I am seeing. That feeling of connection, for some reason, has yet to materialize,

despite the obvious splendor of my surroundings.

Fortunately, things shift profoundly on day three, which brings me to the namesake of this hike: the *torres*, or towers, a set of three granite rock spires that emerge abruptly behind an ice-blue alpine lake. So commanding is their awe-inspiring presence that the entire area and the national park have been named after their grandeur.

Around 5:30 a.m. the morning I am to approach the towers, I quietly leave the hut among the barely perceptible sounds of people stirring from their night of sleep. As I take out my map to confirm my directions, I turn toward the imposing mountain that's just now casting its deep-gray shadow in the slated early morning light. I start my climb. Gently, the sky above me transitions from the tentative light of dawn to a thick white haze that envelops both the valley where I walk and the mountain that houses my destination. There is a very real chance that the fog will thicken to a total whiteout and obliterate any chance of seeing the towers. I know I will be deeply disappointed to have come all this way and not witness what makes this park so famous. But if there's one thing I've learned while traveling, it's that being attached to a particular experience or outcome is never beneficial. So many times I have laboriously worked my way up to a mountain summit only to find the entire view shrouded in white. Or I have begun a multiday adventure filled with the promise of stunning vistas only to end up slogging through endless rain. Being a hiker is a particularly effective way to practice the art of letting go, because being disappointed by what you do not see will only diminish your ability to find gratitude for what is actually there.

The trail toward the *torres* is a lovely ascent, and at that early hour, I am the only person making this pilgrimage. Since Sarah spent the previous evening in a hut higher up on the mountain, I stop there hoping to share a cup of coffee while I warm my hands and feet. I look for her familiar teal shirt but see only strangers seated around me.

A light snow is falling when I get back to the trail, and I turn my face upward to feel the snowflakes land softly on my cheeks, chin, nose, and eyelids. As I return my gaze to the trail ahead, I see a familiar bright-blue shirt silhouetted against the snowy backdrop. When I catch up with Sarah, her blonde eyelashes are dusted with tiny snowflakes—the colorlessness of the crystals against the lightness of her complexion gives her a look both fairy-like and mystical.

"There's no view up there," she says, and I sense the heaviness of her disappointment. "Just a whiteout. I didn't see the *torres* at all."

I tell Sarah how sorry I am and that we should absolutely talk more about it over a beer that night (we've both fallen in love with the local Austral beer and have declared every day on trail a reason to celebrate with one of the delicious varieties). While Sarah turns to continue her hike back down to the main trail, I push on. Above me, I can see the slightest strip of blue, which is all the motivation I need to hold on to hope that the towers will show themselves by the time I reach the viewpoint.

Eventually, the soft dirt trail leads to a boulder field where instead of blazes on trees, red bullseyes are painted on rocks to indicate the route. Yet in the thick of the fog, I struggle to find my way, and more than once, I get lost among the large rocks before finding the trail again. But the snow is no longer falling, and in its place, there's an ever-so-slight opening of blue against the whiteness of sky. I fervently send every ounce of energy and positive intention into that sliver, hoping that enough of the clouds will clear to allow the *torres* to emerge.

As I sidestep the last boulders between me and the towers, I notice the energy change. It is a subtle shift, as if the mundane has been sweetly infused with a bit of the divine. I walk by car-size boulders that seem to stand guard for the precious landscape just beyond. The fabled towers. When I arrive, they are still cloaked in a silky cloud, but little by little, their stark granite outline is revealed against the white veil of mist. I look around and spot just one solitary hiker sitting at the edge of the glacial lake that separates the towers from where I stand.

I am transfixed.

Arriving here is like stepping into another world. The air feels different, and my sense of time is arrested. Typically when I reach a hiking goal, I quickly turn around to chase the next milestone, but here I am without movement. I sit with solemn reverence at the water's edge and pause for I don't know how long. The clouds feel like an invitation to practice mindfulness, and as they slowly shift, my longing to view the towers in their full majestic presence deepens.

I wait.

My body feels paralyzed with the anticipation of seeing the three rock formations. I find a synchronized rhythm with my breathing as I sit in this vortex of time, watching each small shift in cloud cover.

I wait.

An hour slips by. My body is cold, and my joints begin to stiffen. But nothing in me wants to abandon the possibility of seeing the towers, so I breathe through the discomfort.

And then it happens.

For less than one minute, the bank of clouds parts to reveal a blue sky, and all three towers stand clearly before me. Their presence brings to mind the energy of elders, those who have protected this land for thousands of years. I sit mesmerized, absorbing each crevice and angular line of these three beautiful gifts. And then, as quickly as they separated, the clouds reclaim the towers as their own. The spell lifts, and I realize I have stayed as long as I had been invited. I lift my pack onto my back, and return to the journey of the trail.

LOGISTICS

This hike can easily be completed solo or with a group. The main advantage of booking with a group is to get help navigating the accommodation booking system, which can be challenging. If you have the will to wrangle a variety of websites for bookings, going solo is definitely an option. I loved doing this hike on my own.

Choosing a Route

There are two main routes through the Torres del Paine. The first is the W route, which is about fifty miles long and can be completed in three to five days. It covers some of the most iconic highlights in the park: Grey Glacier, Frances Valley, and the famous *torres* themselves. On the W route, you can stay in mountain huts the entire way, but do note that in high season, it tends to be very crowded.

The O circuit covers the same trail as the W but is eighty-five miles long and generally completed in eight or nine days. On this route, you'll spend two or three nights camping in the less-traveled rear of the park, which offers more solitude and greater opportunities to see varied terrain. This is a harder route and the one I took, but the views and solitude are worth it!

Getting to the Trailhead

Most people begin their journey to Patagonia by flying into either Santiago, Chile, or Buenos Aires, Argentina, and taking a connecting flight to Punta Arenas, Chile. From Punta Arenas, you'll take a roughly three-and-a-half-hour bus ride to Puerto Natales, the gateway town to Parque Nacional Torres del Paine. There are a lot of bus companies running this route, but it's always a good idea to buy a ticket ahead of time. You can research travel options by looking up "BusBud" or "Recorrido." The adorable town of Puerto Natales has tons of lodging options where you can get a good night's rest before your first day on trail.

From Puerto Natales, you'll take a ninety-minute bus ride to the Torres del Paine on the day you plan to begin your hike. You can either buy this bus ticket online or at the bus station in town.

Length and Difficulty

Depending on which route you choose, this hike can last five to ten days. The hardest day on either trail is on the O circuit, hiking over John Gardner Pass. Not only is this stretch physically demanding, it can be further complicated as the pass is sometimes closed due to poor weather. However, the view from the summit is one that you'll remember for a lifetime.

Accommodations

The mountain huts on this hike are known as *refugios*. These simple lodges have bunk beds in mixed dormitories and often feature shared bathrooms with showers and hot water, a restaurant and bar, and living rooms that are generally heated. Three separate companies operate the mountain huts, and as I've mentioned, it can be pretty labor intensive to figure out how to book your accommodations (this was the most stressful part of the trip for me). I do recommend visiting the Patagonia Dreaming website, which has a great guide to help you plan your hut reservations.

As an alternative, you can save money by tent camping throughout your hike.

Best Time to Hike

It is recommended to hike the Torres del Paine from December through February thanks to longer days and better weather.

Pro Tips

Leave your hut super early, despite the warnings about puma encounters! Since the W route is so crowded, if you want solitude on trail, it's better to pack your breakfast for a later picnic and put some miles in soon after sunrise.

I loved the food in Chile, and there are so many delightful items to take home with you! If you like your food on the spicier side, then I absolutely recommend picking up the spice *merkén*. If you're a beer drinker, their local brand Austral is fantastic. And know that if you're offered to share a yerba maté by someone on trail, this is a sweet sign of friendship.

Finally, if you enjoy a good distillery, Last Hope, the southernmost distillery in the world, is located in Puerto Natales. Consider treating yourself to a delicious gin or mixed cocktail at the end of your epic hike.

BOOK

Torres del Paine: Trekking in Chile's Premier National Park by Rudolf Abraham (Cicerone Press Limited).

LOCAL LANGUAGE: SPANISH

Thank you: Gracias (GRAH-sea-ahs)
Please: Por favor (pour FAH-vor)
I'm sorry: Lo siento (low SEA-en-toe)

REGIONAL RECIPE

Of all the mountain huts I've stayed in during my travels, the *refugios* in Patagonia served up the most delicious food. Here's a hearty stew recipe that is quite enjoyable after a day of hiking up mountains and around glaciers.

CHILEAN BEAN STEW

(Porotos Granados)

Serves 4–6

INGREDIENTS

1 tbsp olive oil

1 ½ tsp smoked paprika

½ tsp chili flakes

1 small yellow onion, finely chopped

2 cups butternut squash, cut into ½-inch cubes

2 cups frozen corn

3 tomatoes, diced

2 cups vegetable broth

salt and pepper to taste

1 ¼ tsp cumin

2 (15 oz) cans cannellini beans

¼ cup of fresh basil, whole

DIRECTIONS

1. Heat 1 tbsp of oil in a medium saucepan over medium-high heat. Once hot, add paprika and let cook for 1 minute. Add onion and cook until translucent, about 5 minutes.

2. Add butternut squash, corn, tomatoes, and vegetable broth to the pan, along with salt, pepper, cumin, and fresh basil. Cook covered on medium heat for 15 minutes.

3. During this time, drain and wash beans. Add them to the covered pot after 15 minutes until they are heated. Once the dish is ready to serve, remove the basil and enjoy!

The Dingle Way

May 2018

DIFFICULTY: Easy | LENGTH: **111 miles (178 km)** | ELEVATION GAIN: **13,435 feet (4,095 m)** | DURATION: **8–9 days**

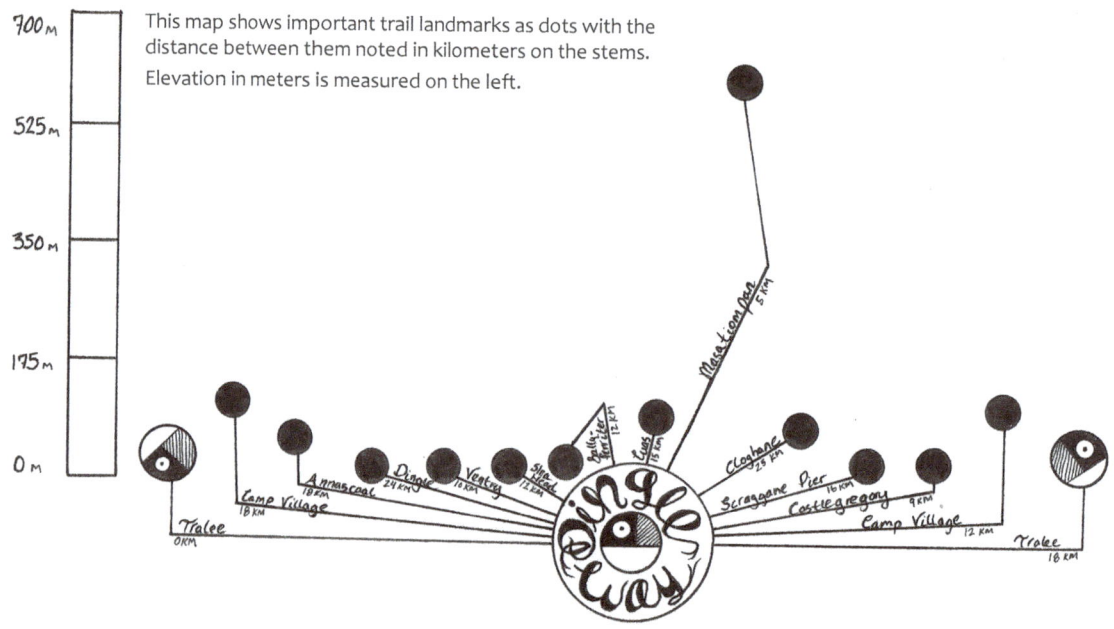

This map shows important trail landmarks as dots with the distance between them noted in kilometers on the stems.

Elevation in meters is measured on the left.

In nature, nothing is perfect and everything is perfect. Trees can be contorted, bent in weird ways, and they're still beautiful.

—ALICE WALKER

  LESSON... **Find your own adventure.**

My feet are sopping wet. And not the type of wet that's well-deserved after navigating a particularly gnarly river crossing or trekking toward a peak through unbroken knee-deep snow. They're the type of wet that comes after a day of trudging along unrelenting muddy trails through disconsolate cow farms. My vegan sensibilities continually cringe as I hear live cattle screaming in anticipation of what is most likely an imminent and early demise. Their panicked cries echo loudly off the walls of the dilapidated farm buildings surrounding me.

I do not like this hike at all.

I chose the Dingle Way after my friend Hilary and I decided on Dublin for our "D" year of travel. Our fabulous alphabet strategy (which lives on today) started organically four years prior with a birthday trip to Austin, followed by my friend's visit to my home in Asheville later that same year. The "A" of those cities prompted an idea that we agreed would guide our next twenty-five adventures. Over wine at an outdoor cafe, we decided that every year moving forward, we'd choose the next letter in the alphabet and plan a trip around a town, city, state, or country that started with that letter. Our goal was to designate places that were a bit off the beaten path, a bit out of our comfort zones, a bit different from the typical tourist destinations.

So why we agreed on Dublin for our "D" trip after amazing adventures in Bali and Croatia was a bit unclear to me. In truth, it was Hilary who was particularly excited about Ireland because of its history and beauty. When advocating for this destination, she appealed to my love of whiskey, reminding me repeatedly of the distilleries that dot the Irish countryside. Though I had visited (and not particularly enjoyed) Dublin when I studied abroad in England my junior year at university, that was twenty years ago, so I assumed Dublin would offer a much different experience this time around.

It did not.

Dublin is wonderful if you enjoy European cities with winding cobblestone streets, historic buildings that house museums and pubs, and the sound of live music spilling out onto the sidewalks. And while Dublin is infused with the sweet symbiosis of contemporary style and historical relevance, for me, the longer I live in the mountains, the more I prefer swapping out busy streets for quiet trails. To put it succinctly, cities and I have had our moment, called it quits, and happily gone our separate ways.

Knowing that time spent in an urban setting would leave my heart and my legs

hungry for dirt paths and fresh air, I scoured the internet before my departure to identify a local hike that would prove challenging, aesthetically pleasing, and full of opportunity for the isolation I treasure. After much research, I decided the Dingle Way—a trail around the Dingle Peninsula on Ireland's southwest Atlantic coast—would be that hike. Its unique beauty featuring mountain paths that give way to seaside trails and craggy cliffs was not something I commonly found when hiking throughout the world. Adding to this allure was *National Geographic Traveler* magazine's declaration that the Dingle Peninsula was "the most beautiful place on earth."
How could I not be tempted?

After saying goodbye to my friend at the conclusion of our lackluster Dublin adventure, I am ready to head out solo to start my hike. I'm excited—a sentiment fueled by the enjoyable warm-up hike I took the day before on the southern coast of the Dingle Peninsula. I traded the town of Dingle, a charming ocean community with a famous local dolphin and a damn good distillery, for the smaller town of Annascaul. This sweet pastoral village's claim to fame is a darling pub that houses a makeshift museum dedicated to Tom Crean, an Annascaul native who'd made Ireland proud during his daring pursuits with the Antarctic explorer Ernest Shackleton in the early 1900s. I enjoyed my quick walk through the touching tributes at the museum before leaving the pub to explore the town's surrounding mountains on foot.

The trail I chose, called the Three Peaks of Annascaul, had an aesthetic that can only be described as haunting. The green swaths of treeless mountains, with barely a hint of discernible path, wove around algae-filled lakes and barren fields. I worked my way up an old dirt road toward the mountain summit, admiring the endless views surrounding me. The quality of the quiet there was unbelievable, with just the occasional birdsong layered on top of the gentle wind percussion.

This place was stunning.

Everything in the mountains of Annascaul felt different from the hikes I had done before. Even the various hues of green were delightfully unfamiliar to me. Unlike the mountains I typically hike, with craggy rock spires reaching vertically into the sky, here the stones had unusual shapes, jutting out unpredictably at odd angles from hidden crevices. As I approached the summit, a fog-like mist hung languorously along the ridge, and when I reached the top, the clouds swirled delicately around the surrounding peaks as if gently caressing their ragged limestone edges.

In a moment somewhat out of character for me, I paused at the top, sat quietly, and just listened to the silence. It felt strange to not immediately turn around and leave the summit for the comfort of a hot shower waiting below, but something here felt too precious, too divine, too special to leave so quickly.

Below me, flocks of sheep milled around a field. Some were painted with splashes of hot pink, others adorned with patches of bright blue. From my perspective, they looked like slow-moving candy pieces as they lazily grazed. Above, the sun sat hazy in the midday sky, and I found myself falling in love with Ireland.

But that changed once I began walking the Dingle Way.

After leaving my rustic bed-and-breakfast in Annascaul, I set out on day one with high hopes, bravely marching onto the trail in the gray, misty Irish morning. Though I knew the conditions would be muddy at best and perhaps a bit frustrating at worst, I thought I was prepared to endure mud-encrusted pants and dirty shoes for the payoff of seeing stunning beaches and the scenery that had inspired Irish ballads.

The first day of a hike is often a poor representation of the journey to follow. During the initial stretch, you frequently cover less interesting ground to reach the truly pretty places. First days tend to feel like a warm-up for the main show, and it's often necessary to put in quite a number of mediocre miles to get to the knock-your-socks-off scenery. I try to keep this in mind as I walk along the endless paved roads and muddy footpaths of this stretch of the Dingle Way as it heads through thorny briars and monotonous farmland. It is plain and ugly. Not only that, it's smelly. And sadly, I hate it.

Let's talk a bit about the mud on the Dingle Way. This isn't the type of mud that simply creates small halos around the soles of your shoes and changes the color of your sneakers into a yucky shade of brown. It's not even the type of mud that makes your feet look like disfigured, crusty clown shoes. The mud of the Dingle Way is the type that fuses to your shoes and exerts great oppositional force as you try to lift your foot with each encumbered step. The kind of mud that finds its way inside footwear and socks and adds burdensome amounts of weight that can hamper an already challenging hike. And the mud here not only smells bad, but no matter the daytime temperature, it never seems to dry out.

The trail miles on the Dingle Way are filled with these conditions: mud, farms, screaming cows, and the occasional view of a sheep pasture. I am bored and also dismayed by how much of this journey involves walking on pavement. Heat mercilessly radiates from the scorching asphalt as I take step after step, quickly losing hope that anything beautiful awaits me on this trek.

But then, to my surprise, I occasionally have the pleasure of encountering a castle.

These moments are, admittedly, quite spectacular. While hiking in the mountains of North Carolina, I might stumble upon old, rusted cars and moonshiners' stills lying hidden in the mountain foliage. But by contrast, in Europe, it's entirely possible to come across ancient cathedrals, towering fortresses, and the remnants of regal medieval castles while on a hiking trail. Often, these ancient structures are in some stage of being reclaimed by the trees and plants that surround their walls, which lends an eerie ambiance. The Dingle Way is home to a surprising number of ruined castles, and they feel to me like beautiful gifts that interrupt the monotony of green.

Day three of my hike brings me to the ocean and an expanse of sandy beach that stretches for miles. I much prefer the sound of the waves lapping against the shore to the frightened cattle cries, and I find the uneventful seaside miles soothing. Eventually, beach transforms into craggy cliffs, and as I walk along the ocean

path, I experience a moment when awe replaces boredom, and gratitude replaces ennui. It's that lovely time when walking and wonder merge to form cherished memories. These steps along the coastal path feel like an arrival for me. Now I understand—this is why I came to Ireland.

Sadly, the next day, the trail leads me back to mud and farmland. At one point, I try to create my own adventure by going off trail to hike up a rogue mountain, only to find myself face-to-face with a herd of what seem to be extraordinarily unfriendly sheep who begin to circle me in an oddly aggressive fashion. I fear I may have seriously compromised my physical safety with my off-trail decision and can see no way around the contingent of potentially murderous sheep. Were it not for the ringing of a food bell and the sheeps' corresponding Pavlovian response to dash away to dinner, I might not be here to share this tale. I seize the moment to quickly slip through a metal gate back to safety.

The final day on the Dingle Way brings me to the base of Mount Brandon, the highest peak on the Dingle Peninsula at 3,122 feet. I'm so happy to see an actual trail up an actual mountain! As soon as my feet touch the dirt that morning, I feel as if I've regained a part of myself that has remained largely dormant during this walk. I am exhilarated with a sense of expansiveness as I begin my ascent through the unearthly terrain, with its rocky outcrops and crater-like lakes. My trail notes direct me to hike up to the mountain's shoulder and return downhill into town, but I am not one to turn my back on the opportunity to reach a summit when it's within sight. I abandon my route notes and head up.

As has been true with most of my hiking in Ireland, the trail up to the top of Brandon seems more like the suggestion of a path than a clear indication. But as luck would have it, I am attempting my summit on the same day that a local charity is hosting a fundraising hike leading to the top of the mountain. Not only are there bright yellow flags that clearly outline the correct path, but spectators lining the trail cheer me on as I climb the last few miles. I notice that they repeatedly mistake me for a woman named Julie and express humored confusion when I thank them for their words of encouragement in an American accent. Were it not for their goodwill and the convenient marking of the path, I might not have made my summit that day.

Eventually, I reach the top and pass through the joyous celebration, walking among sweaty, happy hikers who take photos arm-in-arm and gulp down granola bars and sports drinks. Their laughter has a contagious quality, and I smile as I walk among their congratulatory hugs and smell their stinky clothes. Though these hikers will likely return the same way they ascended, I have mapped out a circular route for my journey back and will descend via a less frequented trail on the other side of the mountain.

As soon as I leave the group and begin my descent, everything in the landscape goes silent. This shift in both the energy and the surroundings is sudden and disorienting for me, and for a moment, I find my feet unable to move forward as my eyes take in the glorious panorama in front of me. Numerous reflective pools of bright green and deep blue dot the mountainside. It is nothing short of magical, and I quicken my pace to reach the part of the trail that weaves through this watery wonderland. The silence is soul-nourishing, and the atmosphere enchanting. After five days of being spiritually lost, I feel like myself again: joyful, curious, strong, grateful. There is an elation as I move through Brandon's boulder fields and moss-filled valleys. I revel in the singular allure of this landscape and take in deep breaths of pure mountain air. It has been a tough adventure, but this moment alone makes it all worthwhile. All I really needed was to witness the hidden beauty of one mountain, in one moment, in one land. Perhaps I do not hate Ireland after all.

LOGISTICS

Choosing a Route

The Dingle Way is traditionally walked in a clockwise direction, starting from Tralee and branching south at Camp Village. The trail passes through the town of Dingle before making the journey around Slea Head and looping back across the north of the Dingle Peninsula.

Getting to the Trailhead

To get to the Dingle Way, fly into Dublin or Shannon and take a train or bus to the town of Tralee where the official hike begins. You can also fly from Dublin or Shannon to Kerry Airport, which will put you twelve miles from the town of Tralee. The trail begins directly from Tralee town center.

However, you can also do a shorter route, as I did, and begin in the town of Annascaul. To get maps of each stage of the hike, visit the official website for the Dingle Way.

Length and Difficulty

The walk is a circuit around the Dingle Peninsula and starts and finishes in Tralee. The trail is 111 miles long and takes an average of eight to nine days to walk its entirety. However, you can arrange a shortened trip by hiring a shuttle service. It is a fairly easy trail to hike.

Accommodations

The Dingle Way winds through the center of many picturesque villages and towns. It's easy to find restaurants along the trail, and there are a plethora of local bed-and-breakfasts to choose from. It's always recommended to arrange your lodging ahead of time. If you want your luggage transferred so you can be free to carry only a light pack, book this service through a travel agency. I used MACS Adventures, who arranged all of my accommodations and luggage transfers.

Best Time to Hike

The Dingle Way can be hiked between April and October, but be prepared for wet conditions anytime of year.

Pro Tips

My feet got so muddy and wet during my time on the Dingle Way that it seriously detracted from my enjoyment. In retrospect, I wish I'd brought a waterproof anti-slip shoe cover, which would have made the hiking more pleasant.

Also, remember to bring snacks! Though there are many towns along the route, there are long stretches without amenities.

BOOKS

Dingle Way by Sandra Bardwell (Rucksack Readers).

The Dingle Peninsula: A Walking Guide by Adrian Hendroff (Collins Press).

REGIONAL RECIPE

Nothing warms you up after a day of hiking through the Irish fog like a delicious stew.

VEGAN IRISH STEW

Serves 4–6

INGREDIENTS

1 medium carrot, chopped

½ medium yellow onion, sliced

2 large garlic cloves, minced

½ medium red pepper, chopped

2 tbsp of olive oil

15–20 small mushrooms, chopped

1 cup dry pearl barley

½–1 cup cooked or canned chickpeas

1 tsp cumin

splash of Tabasco sauce to taste

salt and pepper to taste

1 tbsp Bragg Liquid Aminos or soy sauce

3–4 cups vegetable stock

DIRECTIONS

1. In a large soup pot, sauté carrots, onions, garlic, and peppers in oil over medium heat until onions are translucent.

2. Add mushrooms and sauté until mushrooms become tender.

3. Add barley, chickpeas, cumin, vegetable stock, Tabasco, salt, pepper, Braggs, and stock; cover and bring to a boil.

4. Option: add some vegan sausage for a more textured/hearty stew!

5. Reduce heat, remove the lid, and simmer for 20–30 minutes, until barley is cooked.

Kumano Kodo

June 2018

DIFFICULTY: Hard | LENGTH: **444 miles (71 km)** | ELEVATION GAIN: **7,480 feet (2,280 m)** | DURATION: **4–5 days**

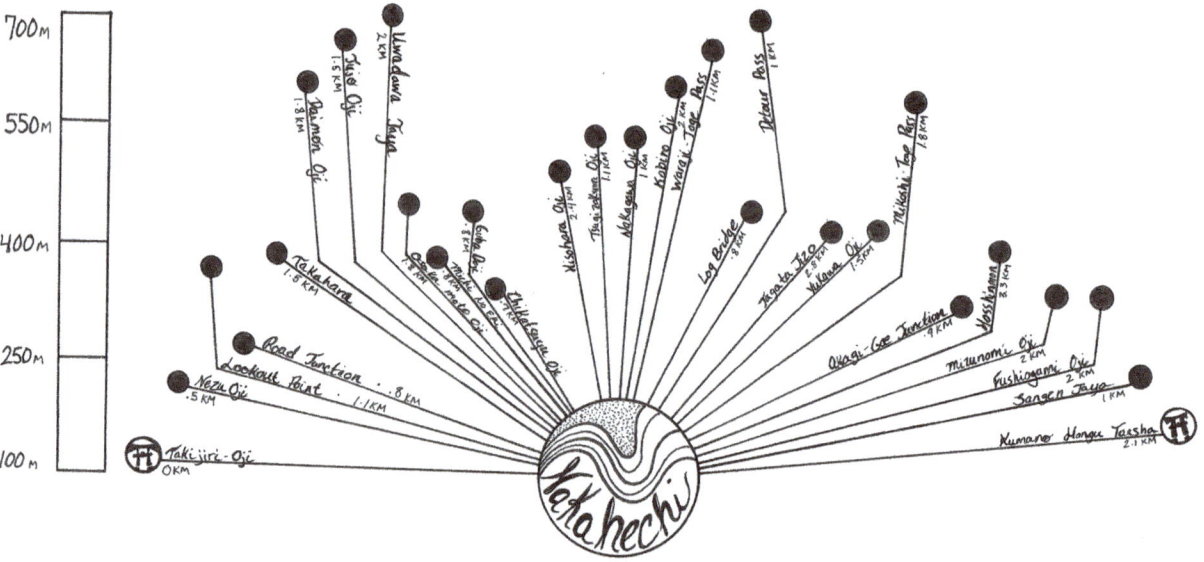

This map shows important trail landmarks as dots with the distance between them noted in kilometers on the stems. Elevation in meters is measured on the left.

*You can never conquer the mountain,
you can only conquer yourself.*

—JIM WHITTAKER

●●●● LESSON... Find your gratitude moment. ●●●●

I have boarded a small bus in the town of Tanabe, having just completed a train ride that hugged the liminal space where mountain meets sea in southern Japan. Aside from those on the bus that call this area home, there is one solitary American family of four sitting directly in front of me, eating bags of processed food and occupying more energetic space than their numbers would suggest. I have no doubt that they too are traveling to the sacred pilgrimage of the Kumano Kodo.

When we exit the bus, I do my best to push past the Americans to get to the trailhead first and enjoy my coveted solitude. But alas, I am not quick enough. They immediately create a significant roadblock at the head of the trail. I try to politely pass one family member at a time while pushing up the surprisingly steep ascent, hiding the fact that I'm already dramatically winded by smiling at each person as I leapfrog past them. It takes effort, but eventually, I find myself gloriously alone on this holiest of trails. It is now time for my journey to truly begin.

I first heard about the Kumano Kodo in an article deeming it the most beautiful pilgrimage you've never heard of. Having completed the Camino Frances a few years before, I was in love with the idea of becoming a pilgrim once again. Add to that the bonus of visiting Japan—to see its sacred temples and manicured gardens bursting with color, to bear witness to its introspective Buddhist culture, and to taste its famous whiskey—and it did not take long before I found myself once again on a plane.

Of the countless mountain treks throughout the world, only a few are designated "pilgrimages," and of those, only two have been named UNESCO World Heritage Sites. One is the Camino de Santiago, and the other is the Kumano Kodo. In fact, pilgrims who complete both the Camino and Kumano are eligible to receive a special certificate and decorative textile to commemorate the accomplishment.

The Kumano Kodo's rich history spans more than a thousand years. Academic records reveal that it was the pilgrimage site of spiritual seekers, emperors, and samurais in ancient times, and its sacredness can be felt energetically throughout its twists and turns. The massive forest trees seem like old souls who chose nature as their reincarnated life form, standing in tribute to the path that resonated so deeply with them in past times. This sensation of reincarnated energies is also present in the odd assortment of creatures I meet along the way: pencil-thin snakes, luminous blue crabs, centipedes with neon-red legs, vibrant spiders spinning thick-roped webs, and kaleidoscopic-colored birds that skim the tops of the tall pines. With all of the history embedded in this footpath, it's not surprising that the spiritual aspirations of ancient pilgrims seem to infuse the living plants and animals around me.

Other than the family that I thankfully encountered only on my first day, the trail is almost uniformly silent and devoid of other hikers. I consistently see only one fellow pilgrim, and other than our occasional meetings on trail and the evening meals we share, I am alone. It is completely glorious. I get this physical sensation when I hike for days in sweet solitude: it's as if every cell in my body is vibrating with a joyous hum, and my spirit feels elevated from this blissful energy.

I become the most present and grateful version of myself.

On the Kumano Kodo, my sense of awe and renewal is deepened by the spiritual temples and the relics placed in the hidden crevices of these mountains. There are ancient shrines and statues housed throughout the forest canopy, and each day I find myself stopping to reflect and meditate near these powerful religious artifacts. Their energetic resonance, coupled with the stillness here, is stunning.

The trail ventures deep into the forests where the trees stand in tall columns that stretch boldly between earth and sky. Unlike the dramatic lush landscape of my home in North Carolina, where branches and roots create intricate mosaics along mountain paths, here the trees are organized and upright. I find comfort in their dependability and uniformity.

It's day three of my trip, and rain arrives in the steady torrential downpour often associated with spring. My rain gear is impotent against the force of wind and water, and I surrender to the cold and wet as I walk the undulating trail. Part of me feels discouraged. The relentlessness of the rainstorm quickly dampens my spirit as I contemplate the many miles of wet hiking that lie before me.

And then something in me shifts.

For one moment, I stop scanning the soggy trail for the slick rocks and jutting roots that could easily cause a sprained ankle. Instead, I look up. Even with the sheets of rain obscuring the forest around me, I see a soft fog encasing the treetops that transforms my sodden surroundings into an artistic masterpiece. It is a sacred moment—a connection to the wonder of where I am.

In my mind, I hear that soft whisper of an insight that has preceded every dot tattooed on my wrist. That divine guidance that brings me back to the trail time and time again. Today the lesson is strong and clear: find gratitude in this moment. Despite the rainstorm. Despite the cold. Despite the exhaustion and dreariness, the soaked clothes and sloshing shoes—find gratitude. And I simultaneously remember and know that it is when magic is most hidden that gratitude is the strongest force for transformation. In this moment, deep within a forest in Japan, something in me changes. It's as if the ancient wisdom of this land has shared a truth so simple and profound that I somehow become more spacious inside.

On day four, I see the ocean for the first time. I am ascending my last significant climb, and though I am feeling strong, I am humbled by two local women, easily twice my age, who pass me effortlessly (in flip-flops) and set up their picnic reward by the time I reach the mountain's summit. They have a sweet, easy laughter and greet me with smiles informed by the wisdom that comes with age and a dedication to living full lives.

The ocean first reveals herself in a clearing between tree groves on the summit. On the horizon, mountain peaks gradually shrink in size and stature as they make their way down to the shoreline. From where I stand, I can just make out the white crests on the waves as they shift among the rocky outcrops offshore. Getting to this point means that my end goal is near—to

reach the Kumano Hongu Taisha Grand Shrine. A photo of this temple was what first ignited my intense desire to walk this trail, and now, knowing that I am so close feels intoxicating.

My pace picks up significantly as I quickly move downhill, first through forest, then meadow, then town, then back to forest, and at last I am there. The fairytale splendor of this area is more awe-inspiring than any camera could capture. I have arrived at *Seiganto-ji* (青岸渡寺), the Temple of Crossing the Blue Shore. The red and green pagoda stands proudly against the backdrop of the Kii Mountain Range and Nachi Falls, the country's tallest uninterrupted waterfall.

Tourists equipped with cameras and eager smiles exit large buses, waiting to see the ancient shrine hidden in the mountain's depth. They all look fresh and smell good and seem to have more energy than my dwindling reserves to walk up and down the curving paths of the holy site. I quickly become aware of my dirty clothes and muddy shoes as I join them and try to blend in as I wander in and out of holy buildings where we are enveloped in the scent of incense and the sounds of monks singing their afternoon prayers.

The longer I remain in the temple complex, the deeper my feeling of tranquility, elevated by the holy energy that infuses the structures around me. After an hour exploring the temples, I walk to the bridge next to the picture-perfect waterfall and let the soft spray gently mist my face and arms. I feel like I could stay here for hours, but eventually, I'm pulled away by the realization that I might miss the last boat shuttle to my hotel on a nearby island. I purchase a T-shirt at the local gift store on my way out, which feels like such a trivial ending to such a momentous journey. No souvenir could come close to honoring what I have learned here. I leave the sacred temples, take a turtle-shaped boat to a kitschy resort close by, and complete my trek by soaking in the hot-spring water from the depth of the mountain. It nourishes my body and heart as this journey ends and creates an internal space for another to begin.

LOGISTICS

Choosing a Route

There are multiple routes you can take to experience a pilgrimage in the southern Kansai region of Japan. I chose the most common and accessible route, known as *Nakahechi*. Information about all of the route options can be found online on the Japan Guide website.

Getting to the Trailhead

I began my trip in Kyoto and took trains and a bus to the start of the Kumano trail. For great step-by-step instructions (accompanied by photos) of how to take public transport to the hike, see the Kumano Kodo guide on the Inside Kyoto website.

Length

The *Nakahechi* route is forty-five miles and typically takes four to five days to complete.

Accommodations

Along the route, you'll stay in traditional Japanese accommodations that are either *ryokan* or *minshuku*. Broadly speaking, *ryokan* are basic inns, while *minshuku* are more akin to bed-and-breakfasts, but almost uniformly, both consist of simple furnished private rooms (some with ensuite bathrooms) with futons on the floor. Bathing occurs in communal gender-specific baths known as *onsen*. Both *ryokan* and *minshuku* serve delicious regional food.

To make logistical planning easier, I hired MACS Adventure to book all my accommodations. When you purchase their self-guided walking trip, they also provide maps and route notes, in addition to arranging all meals.

If you'd prefer to book your own accommodations, check out the information on the Kumano Travel website.

Best Time to Hike

You can hike the Kumano Kodo year-round, though there's a chance of snow in the winter months. Cherry blossoms appear in late March/early April, with fall foliage in October and November. Summer is a lovely time, though potentially hot and humid. The June rainy season can be quite wet, but it doesn't typically rain every day.

Pro Tips

One of the activities I enjoyed about the Kumano Kodo trail was collecting stamps from the sacred sites along the path. At each significant location, you'll find a wooden stand with a stamp and a red inkpad to fill your credential, a type of passport for pilgrims. Credentials can be picked up at the Tanabe Tourist Information Center and the Kumano Travel Support Center near the JR Kii-Tanabe station, the Kumano Hongu Heritage Center near the Kumano Hongu Taisha shrine, and the Kumano Kodo Kan Pilgrimage Center next to Takijiri-oji shrine.

If you've walked the Camino de Santiago, bring proof of completion (a photo of your certificate works) to be certified as a dual pilgrim and receive a special badge at the end of your hike.

BOOKS

Japan's Kumano Kodo Pilgrimage by Kate Davis (Cicerone Press 2019).

LOCAL LANGUAGE: JAPANESE

Thank you: ありがとうございます (AH-RI-gahtoe go-zi-mah-stah)
Please: お願いします (own-AY-GUY-ee-she-ma)
I'm sorry: ごめんなさい (go-MEN NAH-sigh)

REGIONAL RECIPE

Though it was somewhat challenging to find vegan food in Japan, I did enjoy the miso soup served at every meal. It is often made with fish sauce (known as *dashi*), but this is a delicious vegan version.

VEGAN MISO SOUP

Serves 4

INGREDIENTS

3 ½ cups water

½ cup medium or firm tofu, cubed

2 large shiitake mushrooms, chopped (or other mushrooms if shiitake are not available)

1 tbsp dried seaweed, chopped (*hijiki* is best)

3 tbsp miso paste (more or less to taste)

3 stalks green onions, chopped

3 tbsp chopped spinach

1 tsp Bragg Liquid Aminos or tamari

DIRECTIONS

1. In a medium pot, add water, tofu, mushrooms, and dried seaweed and bring to a boil on medium-high heat.

2. Reduce heat and simmer for 5–8 minutes, until mushrooms are tender.

3. Remove from heat; stir in miso, green onions, and spinach; and let sit for another 30 seconds.

4. Add Bragg Liquid Aminos or tamari immediately before serving.

Camino San Salvador and Camino Primitivo

September 2018

SAN SALVADOR: DIFFICULTY: **Hard** | LENGTH: **80 miles (129 km)** | ELEVATION GAIN: **10,022 feet (3,055 m)** | DURATION: **~5 days**

PRIMITIVO: DIFFICULTY: **Hard** | LENGTH: **200 miles (322 km)** | ELEVATION GAIN: **15,044 feet (4,585m)** | DURATION: **~2 weeks**

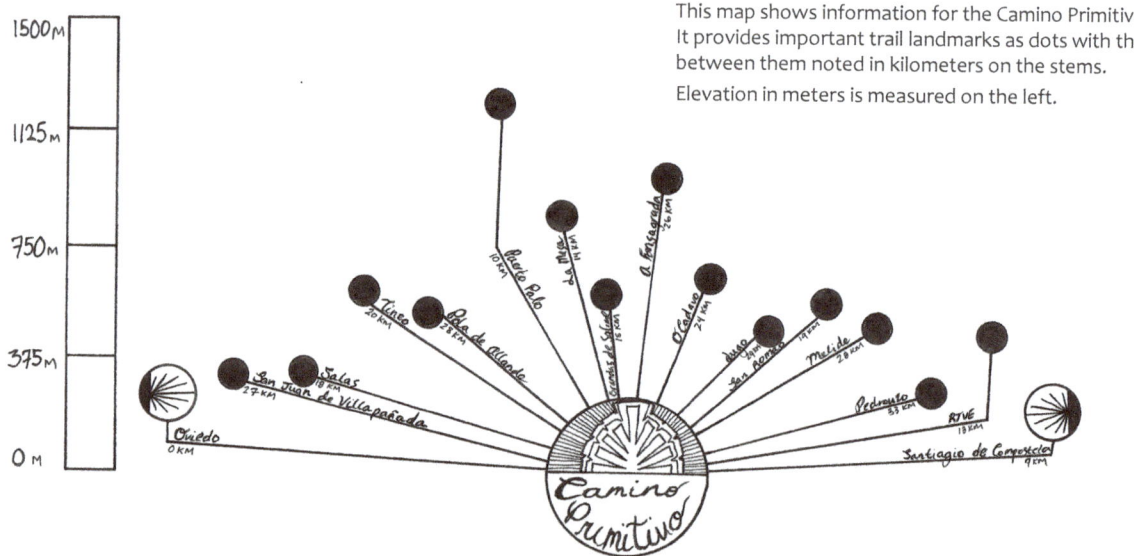

This map shows information for the Camino Primitivo only. It provides important trail landmarks as dots with the distance between them noted in kilometers on the stems.

Elevation in meters is measured on the left.

*Ordinarily I go into the woods alone,
with not a single friend, for they are all smilers
and talkers and therefore unsuitable.*

—MARY OLIVER

●●● LESSON... on the Camino San Salvador... See with youthful eyes. ●●●

●●● LESSON... on the Camino Primitivo... Pause to honor your needs. ●●●

It started as just a duo. My friend Gina, a fellow Camino enthusiast with whom I'd walked some of the Camino Frances, agreed to join me for two additional Camino routes two years after my first pilgrimage. Planning for this trip felt electric, and just thinking about seeing iconic Camino sites put our hearts into a pitter-patter state of glee. Together, we looked forward to following our beloved shell-shaped blazes and yellow arrows through mountain ranges and medieval towns.

Yet somehow, during the hours spent poring over blogs and books and Camino itineraries, Gina and I began to play with the idea of perhaps inviting others to join our pilgrimage. As veteran walkers had once helped guide our first Camino journeys, we could serve as a catalyst to connect our friends to this trail, helping them experience its spiritual wonder.

Of course, there was a little nagging voice in my head reminding me that, one, I abhor groups and their complicated dynamics, and two, walking alone is my happy place. But after pondering the idea, I overruled how I felt about my past experiences and decided it was time to try a group again. I thought maybe it would be different if I were the leader... maybe my love of the Camino would overcome my awkwardness... maybe I really was better at groups than I gave myself credit for...and maybe, just maybe, this opportunity would be another way for me to embrace the type of self-growth that the Camino so famously provides for those who seek it out.

So it was decided: we would invite others to join our pilgrimage.

It did not take long for our two to become ten. We reached out to our Asheville friends who loved hiking and adventure and also embraced a healthy dose of spirituality. We gathered to hash out different aspects of the route. Gina and I offered our walking participants a "tough love" session where we went through their packs and advised them to jettison anything extraneous. We planned training hikes around town so our group could bond and get comfortable wearing their backpacks. We created route notes and lodging plans to simplify our time on trail. And while all this was happening, we witnessed a group of strangers quickly transform into a team of pilgrims ready and excited for the adventure to come.

Somehow our group also came to include two people about whom I wasn't particularly thrilled. The first was the handsome German man I'd met on my first Camino and with whom I'd shared a delightful evening by the seashore. Our fiery Camino romance had quickly devolved into a long-distance disaster, with quite a few unpleasant encounters and a pretty big blowout when we were last together. As our relationship deteriorated, I found myself frantic to find a graceful exit from the rubble of what had once been between us. Instead of being bold and telling him I thought it best to go our separate ways forever, I offered him the "consolation prize" of joining my Primitivo group. I prayed to every deity I could think of that he'd refuse my offer. He did not.

The other challenging participant was a man named Sean (not his real name) whom I'd also met on my first Camino. Initially, I had been grateful for his company, quick wit, and sharp intellect—he made the hours of trail walking melt away while he shared his commentary on life and recounted humorous stories about other travelers. It wasn't until the last few days of our hike that I realized how much he had awkwardly glued himself to my side, soon making it clear that his intentions were more than platonic. The more I tried to distance myself from him, the more he monopolized my time. I would never have thought of inviting him to join our Primitivo group, but after he saw my Camino plans that I'd shared with an old friend on Facebook, he swiftly invited himself to come along.

As I write these words now, five years wiser, I hope that I will never again acquiesce to uncomfortable situations simply to avoid awkward conversations. I've learned that sometimes it is necessary to hurt someone's feelings to uphold integrity and self-love. But in 2018, I still had some substantial internal mountains to climb around boundaries and self-honoring, which is how these two men regretfully became part of my Camino story. But perhaps had they not joined my group, thus bringing some excruciating lessons to my Primitivo path, I would not possess the clarity and resolve (and updated friendship policies) that I have today. Whatever the case may be, in the end, these lessons were some of the hardest I had to learn, yet also some of the most life-changing.

When people think of the Camino, they often envision the month-long Camino Frances popularized in the movie *The Way*. But actually, there are seven well-established Caminos (Spanish for "routes") that bring pilgrims to the spiritual end point of the church of Santiago de Compostela. This is where Saint James, the patron saint of

Spain, is said to be entombed. The oldest of these routes is the Camino Primitivo. Whereas the Frances is heavily routed through small towns and along paved routes, the Primitivo claims the remote areas of the mountains. People who love hiking love the Primitivo, and I was beyond excited to have a different Camino experience where nature and stillness would take center stage.

Gina and I learned about the second of our two planned Caminos, the Camino San Salvador, through a lucky encounter at a poetry reading at REI. The event, hosted by the region's Camino club, featured a local poet who exquisitely captured the essence of being a pilgrim in all of its layers and complexities. We fell in love with his work immediately.

When we enthusiastically approached him after his reading, gushing our appreciation for his work, he recommended that we walk the Camino San Salvador. This was the first we'd heard of this short, barely walked Camino, and we were instantly intrigued. A Camino that takes only five days? Yes, please! A Camino whose path is almost solely through the mountains? Absolutely! A Camino whose hills and valleys are filled with silence and stillness? Sign us up!

And so we emerged from the poetry reading with what seemed like a flawless plan: to complete not one but two Caminos. First, Gina and I would enjoy some alone time on the San Salvador together, indulging in girlfriend bonding and Camino love. We would then meet the rest of our group in the town of Oviedo five days later to start walking the Primitivo. It was settled. We would leave in early September.

When I finally arrive in Spain, it's evening, and the transforming colors of the sky are gently settling over the streets of León. It has been two years since my feet touched this ancient pathway, and I remember instantly how much my heart feels held by this land. Before I text Gina about my arrival, I pause to take in my surroundings. The town's horizon decorated by the spires of medieval churches. The locals and pilgrims who fill the neighborhood cafes and bars with their banter and laughter. The Spanish air brimming with the scents of sizzling food and the musty clay of the streets and buildings. I am giddy. Being back here, I feel as if a part of me that has lain dormant for two years has come home.

There's a pervasive energy in the towns that line the Camino—a jovial spirit of camaraderie and celebration. For pilgrims, every town is a tangible symbol of the progress they've made toward reaching Santiago de Compostela. And no matter the trials or tribulations faced during the day, the evenings are always a time of connection and joy. León beautifully embodies that Camino essence and is especially impressive as one of the more magnificent medieval cities along the trail. Standing in its central square, I feel transported back to a time of warring crusaders, politicized kings and queens, and religious ferocity. Both the harshness of its history and beauty of its religiosity shine through the stained-glass windows that line the square.

Gina was traveling through France the week before my arrival, and when I spot her in front of the cathedral's main entrance, she possesses the glow of someone alive with the thrill of adventure. We hug with the fervor of two women who have been dreaming of this moment for almost a year. We made it. We're back in Spain. And soon it will be time to walk.

Our first night out, we eagerly order a steaming plate of pimientos de Padrón, a delicious regional dish of blistered Padrón peppers (a cousin of the *shishito* pepper) that's seasoned with the slightest touch of salt. We continue our culinary indulgence with plates of fresh bread, local olive oil, and red wine that flows freely out of a seemingly bottomless carafe. By the time we stumble back to our Airbnb, our bellies and hearts are full, and I say a prayer as I lie down to sleep that the wine's sedative powers will be stronger than my jetlag and frazzled nerves.

Thankfully, morning comes quickly after a night of deep sleep, and I slip effortlessly back into the pilgrim routine I've performed so many times before. I load up my backpack and fasten my scallop shell to the outside to indicate I am a pilgrim. I say goodbye to Gina and begin to walk. Though we'll meet up each night at preselected destinations, our days are for personal reflection with our individual selves, the trail, and the wisdom waiting to be revealed.

Walking out of the bigger cities along the Camino is never scenic or overly enjoyable. Like the larger cities in the United States, the more populated hubs in Spain preserve their city centers for beautiful buildings and historic interest and confine the industrial zones and car dealerships to the outskirts. But even as I leave León's charming medieval structures behind for its factories and massive parking lots, I feel happy and lighthearted. The simple fact of being back here and following the trail's yellow arrows and scallop shells has me elevated. I feel like nothing could dampen my spirit today.

As soon as I begin to walk, I have the sensation that it's been only a matter of days, not years, since I last set out on the ancient trails of Spain. The walking itself is soothing in its familiarity. Yet unlike the crowded Camino Frances, the San Salvador is so very peaceful. It prides itself on empty roads and isolated paths, and I find the quiet refreshing. I pass no one as I walk and later learn that there are only sixteen of us on this Camino route at this particular time. Though daytime encounters with other pilgrims are rare, at night Gina and I find each other and fellow pilgrims in mountain hostels where we congregate at communal tables to share freshly baked bread, regional wine, and stories from our time on trail and our lives back home.

Though I'm overjoyed to be walking the Camino San Salvador and savoring the quiet hours alone, I feel like something is missing. I find the nature around me lovely but not awe-inspiring. In all honesty, it feels a bit underwhelming compared to where I've been recently and what I have seen in mountains throughout the world. I'm thirsting for a "wow" factor but find my surroundings just solidly…okay. After hours of repetitive sights on the trail, I can feel myself slipping into a bit of malaise.

And then I force myself to have a reality check.

I remind myself that not every mountain is going to be the most majestic. Not every trail is going to be the most magical. I accept the fact that the more I hike, the more I will be greeted with "more of the same" or "not as pretty as…." So if I'm going to love walking the world's trails in perpetuity, I need to find a way to maintain an attitude of awe instead of expecting my surroundings to perform that task for me. I realize that I need to create a practice so I do not become "beauty complacent." And I understand that the best way to achieve this as I continue my

hike through the mountains of the Asturias region is to see the world with youthful eyes. It comes to me that when I choose to view my surroundings as if I have never seen a mountain or tree or valley river, then *everything* is a wonder. Everything is new. Everything retains that unique magic that makes the world the singular and wonderful place it is.

I shift my perspective and thus elevate my hike.

It takes less than a week to walk from León to Oviedo, and to get there, we traverse deep gullies, hike over tall mountain summits, and suffer through the banality of industrialized roads and highways. We explore small mountain towns laced with cobblestone roads, drink strong coffee in local cafes, and find tiny churches for a little respite. Within the walls of these churches, I quietly connect to the divine energy that imbues this trail—that universal spirit that seems to embrace all seekers during their pilgrimages. My time in empty church pews provides the reflection I need to integrate the lessons from my journey and to begin processing the sorrowful news I have just received.

My grandmother is dying.

Before I began this trip, I knew there was a strong possibility that she'd transition while I was away. In fact, I questioned whether I should even board the plane and commence my pilgrimage knowing that her ninety-seven years on earth were nearing their completion. But when I allowed myself to move beyond the societal "shoulds" regarding death and tradition, I felt like walking this Camino was the best way to honor the woman that my grandmother was in the world. Buddy, as she was called her entire life, had a simple tagline, which she shared with us during most family dinners and outings: "I was born curious," she would say with a proud smile on her lips and a desire in her eyes—a longing for deeper wisdom, greater adventure, and heightened awareness. There was no "off the beaten path" for my grandmother because every road promised a broader connection to the world, as well as a deeper understanding of humanity.

Though I admired Buddy's adventurous spirit, my grandmother was not an easy person. She could be harsh and critical and held antiquated opinions about the right way people should look and behave. Men were to have shaved faces and wear dinner jackets to restaurants. Women's dresses should fall below the knee and not draw too much attention. Certain silverware went with certain dishes and those dishes only, and bad table manners were unacceptable transgressions. Instead of reading me children's books when I was little, Buddy read me tomes on proper etiquette. To this day, instead of Mother Goose rhymes, I remember such instructional refrains as "Like little ships that sail at sea, I drink my soup away from me."

And yet with all her propriety and staunch adherence to conservative societal norms, my grandmother was a pioneer. No place was too far, too foreign, or too uncomfortable for her. The more a certain location differed from the United States, the deeper her desire was to walk its streets, eat the local food, and breathe in the unique scents. It was my grandmother, as well as my father, who taught me to seek out adventure in my life. They both helped me understand the privilege of exploration and its importance in shaping us as global citizens in an ever-changing (and always-fascinating) world.

As I got older and our roles changed (me as the traveler, grandma the one at home living vicariously through my colorful tales), she eagerly expressed her insatiable curiosity for the places I'd visited or the experiences I'd had. She became my personal travel cheerleader, enthusiastically encouraging me to go farther, experience more, and never allow fear to be a barrier to expansion and adventure.

Though I knew my grandmother's death might happen while I was on the Camino, I felt that rather than sitting with her in a sterile hospital room, waiting for the occasional emergence of consciousness from the depths of her transitional slumber, I would stick with my travel plans. It seemed like the best way to honor a woman whose raison d'être had been to experience all that life had to offer.

And so I continue to walk, leaving behind the Camino San Salvador, and join my friends for the Primitivo.

The Camino Primitivo is truly stunning. The path traverses multiple mountain passes, with views to make even the most seasoned hiker teary with gratitude. Mornings on trail frame the distant vistas against a dawn sky of light blues, silky pinks, and soft oranges. I walk for hours through small medieval towns whose ancient homes feature balconies overflowing with flowers in various shades of red and purple. Amidst this cacophony of color, the cobblestone streets create curving mazes around churches and central squares. And beyond the edge of town, mile upon mile of green hills roll peacefully under cloud-dotted skies.

And yet, in the midst of all this tranquility and mountainous wonder, I'm really struggling. On top of processing my grandmother's imminent transition, each day it becomes increasingly clear that group dynamics are still a challenge for me. It's a truth that's thrown further into relief because Gina, who was supposed to be my co-leader (and emotional support) for this part of the trip, left the Primitivo after two days in favor of a more relaxing experience alone in the south of Spain.

So here I am, stuck in a group of hikers I wish I'd never assembled. Though there are a few lovely women with whom I share some joyous moments, those two difficult men continue to make me extremely uncomfortable. They end up acting blatantly domineering (if not outright mean to me) at times. Adding to the equation, there's an acquaintance from Asheville who takes up an uncomfortable amount of energetic space and also triggers the hell out of me. I become an anxious mess. Occasionally, this anxiety turns into outright panic. I feel like an outsider. I struggle to find my grounding. I truly am flailing. I start to resent the trip, resent the group, resent the Camino.

I call Matt back at home in tears more times than I'd like to admit, and it takes all of my strength to resist leaving the challenges of this experience to return to his loving arms and my regular life in North Carolina.

And then something happens that intensifies my struggle.

I am in a square in the town of Poladura when my mother calls. The time has come. She tells me that my grandmother is no longer conscious and will die very soon. Instead of having a final physical meeting with her, I realize that my closure will have to happen energetically, across the ocean—from a small town deep in the mountains of northern Spain to a hospital bed in cold Chicago. I step into the nearest church and take a seat on a wooden pew. A service has just let out, and I can feel the reverberations from the sung hymns and chanted devotionals. In this quiet space, I wait for my emotions to emerge, but there is nothing. I am not yet ready to grieve.

The next day, I rise early to experience the peace of the empty trail. As I walk, I begin to work out my conflicting emotions. I hike through my anger at having a grandmother who often made me feel inadequate and like a disappointment to her. I walk out the frustration from a lifetime of forced social engagements and ostracizing interactions with "polite society." I move through the pain of not having the type of grandmother who showed up consistently with an open heart and a kind word. And I walk through the sadness. Even with her complexities and sharpness, I still love Buddy. She is still my grandmother. And now I know I will never see her again.

I eventually reach a particularly challenging uphill segment, and as I complete the strenuous push to the top, I am surprised to find myself looking down at clouds congregating below. It is impossible to truly capture what it is like to behold a sea of clouds beneath you. It's as if you're in a surrealist painting but instead of earth below, there's a magic ocean of billowing white. I gasp at the beauty of it all.

That ephemeral moment of wonder.

"Here," I think to myself, "is where I will imagine her, where she will eternally reside in my mind and my heart. Here I will envision her as a weightless essence, forever floating without the struggle of a failing body or a complicated world. Here my grandmother's spirit will exist in my mind without rough edges, without complexity, without pain. Here, among these Spanish clouds, is where I can emotionally lay my grandmother to rest."

And then the real sadness finally wells up inside of me. It is as if the sea of clouds shrouding the trail below has somehow permeated my internal barriers, and the grief comes in tsunami strength. My grandmother is dead, and now I can finally honor the depth of her loss.

As the day progresses and I allow myself to walk with the intensity of my emotions, my sadness eventually transforms into another revelation. I start to think about not only what I will miss about Buddy but also the freedom that comes with her passing. Memories of the countless hurtful family gatherings begin to flood my thoughts—the painful dinners with extended family members and their sharp words and quick ridicule. The public events where I was paraded around like a doll others could admire instead of a

multifaceted person. Those never-ending expectations of how one should appear under the spotlight of high-society examination. On this trail, in this moment, I realize that these painful obligations died with my grandmother. All of these suffocating dynamics evaporated when she took her last breath. With my grandmother's death, a new truth emerges for me: from now on, I get to create a life of emotional safety; I get to choose who sits with me at my table.

Though I'm still four days away from the end of the trail at Santiago de Compostela, this sense of newfound liberation makes my Camino complete. It is easy to depart Spain early to attend my grandmother's funeral, knowing that remaining in the unhealthy group dynamics would be an energetic reference to the challenging role my grandmother played in my life. Leaving the Camino establishes a new path of self-honoring and healthy boundaries. It's somewhat unfamiliar terrain, but I'm ready for the journey.

LOGISTICS

Choosing a Route

The Camino San Salvador and the Camino Primitivo are both clearly established routes. Just follow the yellow arrow blazes and scallop shells to stay on trail. However, I found it helpful to download a Camino app for my phone to identify the route on the rare occasion it was unclear. These apps work without cell service and provide distances to the nearest towns, identify where you can find potable water fountains, and show available lodging. There are multiple apps to choose from, but I really enjoyed using *The Wise Pilgrim*.

Getting to the Trailhead

The Camino San Salvador begins in León, Spain. To reach the trailhead, you can fly into Madrid and then to Asturias Airport. Alternatively, you can take a train from Madrid to Asturias, which takes six hours.

Once in León, the Camino San Salvador begins in the Plaza de San Marcos de León. There you will find the fork with the Camino Frances. Follow signs to the Camino San Salvador and continue along Avenida de los Peregrinos, which follows the course of the Bernesga River.

The Camino Primitivo begins in Oviedo. To reach this city, fly into Asturias and take an ALSA bus from the airport to Oviedo, which takes forty-five minutes. Once in Oviedo, the Camino Primitivo begins in front of Oviedo Cathedral.

Length and Difficulty

The Camino San Salvador is eighty miles long and considered a fairly strenuous hike due to the remoteness of the trail and some significant elevation gain. It takes approximately five days to walk. The Camino Primitivo is 200 miles long and is considered hard. It takes approximately two weeks to walk.

Accommodations

See the previous Camino section.

Best Time to Hike

See the previous Camino section.

Pro Tips

One of the most delightful aspects of walking the Camino is having local restaurants and hotels stamp your credential along the way. Each establishment has its own unique stamp, so by the end of your journey, you'll have a lovely, personalized memento of your time on trail. Make sure to get at least two stamps each day to prove you walked the entire route and receive your certificate at the end of your pilgrimage.

In León, you can obtain your credential at the Albergue de las Carbajalas at the monastery of the Benedictine nuns. It's south of the town center, just steps off the Camino Frances where it enters the city from the south. When you reach the cathedral in Oviedo, you can obtain a document called the *salvadorana* to commemorate your walk.

If you're starting your walk in Oviedo, you can purchase a credential for a few euros at the main cathedral. For additional recommendations, please see the previous Camino section.

BOOKS

The Camino Primitivo: A Wise Pilgrim Guide to the Camino Primitivo from Villaviciosa, through Oviedo, to Santiago de Compostela by Michael Matynka Iglesias (self-published).

The Art of Pilgrimage: The Seeker's Guide to Making Travel Sacred by Phil Cousineau and Huston Smith (Conari Press).

LOCAL LANGUAGE: SPANISH

Thank you: Gracias (GRAH-sea-ahs)
Please: Por favor (pour FAH-vor)
I'm sorry: Lo siento (low SEA-en-toe)

REGIONAL RECIPE

This delicacy is famous in the northwest part of the country, and a piping hot plate of these delicious little salted delights is always a welcome treat after a long day of walking.

SPANISH-STYLE BLISTERED PADRÓN PEPPERS
Serves 4

INGREDIENTS

1 tbsp neutral oil, like canola or grapeseed

12 oz Padrón peppers (*shishito* peppers will work as a substitute)

coarse-ground sea salt to taste

2 tbsp extra virgin olive oil

DIRECTIONS

1. Heat oil over high heat in a cast-iron skillet large enough to fit peppers in a single layer.

2. Once oil is lightly smoking, add peppers.

3. Cook without stirring until peppers become blistered on one side, for about 30 seconds.

4. Flip and stir peppers and continue to cook, turning occasionally, until peppers are well-blistered, tender, and crisp. This should take about 1–2 minutes.

5. Season with salt.

6. Transfer peppers to a serving plate. Drizzle with extra virgin olive oil and sprinkle with more coarse salt. Serve immediately.

Julian Alps

June 2019

DIFFICULTY: Hard | **LENGTH: 37 miles (59 km)** | **ELEVATION GAIN: 9,023 feet (2,750 m)** | **DURATION: 5 days**

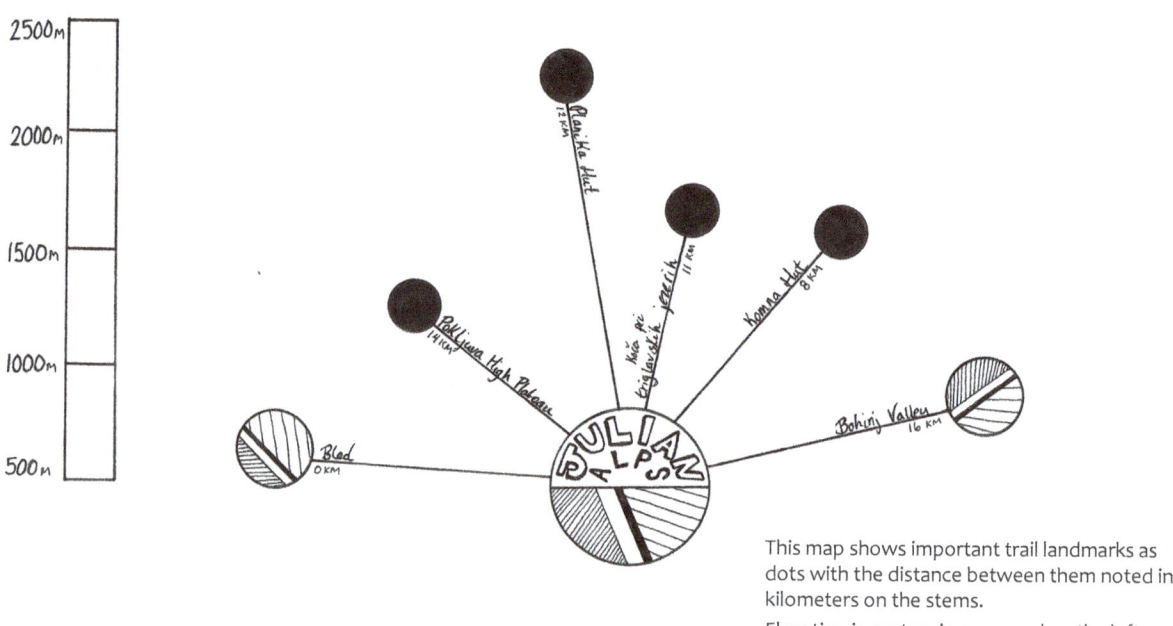

This map shows important trail landmarks as dots with the distance between them noted in kilometers on the stems.
Elevation in meters is measured on the left.

You never conquer a mountain. You stand on the summit a few brief minutes and then the wind blows away your footprints.

—ARLENE BLUM

I have come to this country to hike the famed Julian Alps with their alpine allure and pristine landscapes. Though I land in the capital of Ljubljana, I quickly make my way to the striking shores of Lake Bled. If you have not been to Lake Bled or have never heard of Lake Bled, go. Because it is gorgeous. Sitting on its shores will transform you into the lead character of your own fairy tale with its picture-perfect mountains and charming local architecture.

I feel like I've arrived in a Disneyesque wonderland.

But as I board the boat to see the famous Church of Mary the Queen located on a small island in the middle of the lake, something feels wrong. I check in with my heart to see what this uncomfortable sensation might be and am surprised by what I find: I am lonely. I miss Matt.

Fuck.

We've now been together almost two years, and I have become quite attached to this lovely man. In fact, I often imagine a real future with him. But with that deepened connection has emerged something I've always feared—the sense that my fierce independence might be dulled by the inevitable interdependence inherent in long-term partnership. Until now, I felt completely unencumbered when exploring the world as a solo gal. In fact, at some point I began to see travel *as* my partner. As someone who spent far too many years navigating social engagements and wedding parties with an RSVP of one, I had not previously experienced the type of growth that comes only in relation to an intimate other. I had never stuck around long enough for a romantic partner to expand my worldview by sharing his own with me, to push me out of my comfort zone, or to reflect back to me the contours of my own internal landscape.

I hadn't been aware of the challenge and adventure that partnership could provide.

And so travel became my significant other, consistently pushing me to my limit and forcing me to grow. When I'm alone in foreign countries, I constantly have to navigate the new and unknown—new environments, new languages, new cultures. I've learned how to accept grace when situations go wrong. I have found ways to self-soothe when I feel loneliness or deep disappointment. I get excited to plan my next trip, just like my friends find joy in planning weddings and other partner-oriented celebrations. In travel, I found something to occupy my heart space that continually lifts me up, in the way a significant other might for someone else.

But then Matt somehow found his own trail into my heart and set up residence. And I learned to love traveling with him and creating experiences together. It's been fun to debrief our adventure-filled days over a local whiskey or in a trendy food hall, and I adore staying in quirky lodgings with him (whether it be a cave, yurt, or train caboose) and falling asleep in his arms. I knew even before I met Matt that if I ever found partnership, my travel life would be a mix of "Rachel-only" expeditions and "let's explore this one together" trips. But I never imagined I'd feel the lack of my partner so acutely while traveling on my own.

Fortunately, my Matt-missing moment does not dampen my enjoyment of riding in this wooden boat across this magical lake to a fairy-tale church, but it does make me think about how the way I travel is changing. Most significantly, I am taking fewer solo trips now, which feels appropriate. About nine months into our relationship, Matt reached out to me when I was hiking the Kumano Kodo and told me, "Love, I would never ask you to stop traveling. I know it fills your heart. But I also feel like you are gone a lot. Though I'm not asking you to change, I am naming that it's hard to make something grow when you're absent much of the time."

And after hearing that, while the smallest dissenting voice rose in me to justify my full traveling agenda, I knew he was right. I didn't have to travel in the same way I had before I met him. I recognized that although travel was still my love and my spiritual practice, it was no longer my partner in the world.

Finding a balance between travel and love has been a tough task. The sweet connection that Matt and I experience at home tends to fall off track when I am gone. We're not great at phone conversations, which tend to be awkward and lacking in any natural cadence. And it's hard to feel a connection when one person is having the most amazing time in a far-flung, exotic locale, and the other is dealing with work stress and dog poop and doing all the adulting alone at home. Even on my reentry, our relationship can feel strained; often, it takes a few days before we feel like "us" again.

Matt and I have had to learn to be really intentional with how to make my love of travel work for both of us. Instead of talking on the phone when I'm traveling, we came up with the idea to send each other video messages. I try to be aware of sharing in a way that feels good to us both instead of just gushing about my wonderful experiences abroad. And on his end, Matt works to collect interesting moments from his sometimes monotonous workday to share with me. When I get home, we immediately go on a walk to get reattuned before I am seduced by the pull of mail opening, unpacking, and doing laundry.

I know it's a lot to ask of a partner to be the one holding down the home while I'm off hiking the world, and I'm deeply grateful that Matt keeps showing up in gracious acceptance of this unconventional arrangement. The more I travel, the more my

gratitude grows toward him. And the more I feel Matt's support, the more I want to ask him to join me in these adventures.

These are my thoughts as I start my hike in the Julian Alps. Of all the places I've hiked, I think Slovenia might win one of the top prizes for the greatest beauty. The magnificence of her mountains takes my breath away. I spend the first few days in almost complete solitude as I make my way through wildflower-carpeted meadows, hike among towering trees, and listen to the tinkling music of nearby creeks and rivers. As the trails take me higher, the lushness morphs into the familiar above-the-tree-line moonscape of boulders and granite rock faces speckled in grays and browns. It soon becomes clear that the main summit of the trip is not far.

On my second night, I make it to

Planika Hut, the second-highest lodging in the Julian Alps (with the highest being a mere few hundred feet above). The word "stunning" does not come close to capturing the sublimity that surrounds this small wooden structure. A postcard-perfect motif of towering mountain mastiffs fills the horizon, the peaks extending farther than the eye can see. Having arrived at the hut early, I take countless videos for Matt and friends and just marvel at my surroundings. The amazement holds my focus for hours.

When I originally booked this hike, I was told that I could add the ascent of Triglav, the highest peak in Slovenia, to my itinerary but that the assistance of a guide was mandatory to safely ascend the *via ferrata* (Italian for "iron path"), the climbing route consisting of steel rungs that leads to the mountain summit. Of course, I signed up.

But as other guests arrive at Planika, I quickly realize that none of them have hired a guide to help reach the summit the next morning. I'm acutely embarrassed that I will be the only person using support to climb the peak.

As I sit alone at dinner lamenting the choice to hire help, I get a call from my guide who's still at home and speaks to me with legitimate disappointment.

"I am so sorry," he says. "The weather tomorrow is supposed to be terrible. The conditions will be too treacherous, and the views will be nonexistent. I know you'll be disappointed, but I just do not think it's safe to go."

I feign a sad tone, thank him for letting me know, and immediately go to reception to see if they have safety equipment I can rent. They do. Then, fighting to overcome my overwhelming shyness, I ask two lovely men from the States if I can ascend with them in the morning. I can. I am ready and excited, and 4:00 a.m. cannot come soon enough.

When the communal room of sleeping hikers starts to fill with an orchestra of varied alarm sounds, we groggily begin to assemble our gear and help each other into uncomfortable harnesses. While I am waiting outside for the others to get ready, the sun is just beginning to rise. The sky is as clear as any I have seen thus far in Slovenia. Intense streaks of red and orange light start to fade the starry night above. Fortunately, the guide's weather forecast was incorrect, and it is perfect outside. Eventually, my fellow American travelers and a group of younger Scandinavian women form a line, and together we start to make our way up to Triglav's summit.

There's a popular T-shirt in Slovenia with the bold statement, TRIGLAV: ONLY 4 BRAVE. It doesn't take long to understand why. The hike up to the summit mostly follows an extremely narrow and harrowing ridgeline that's riddled with oddly shaped boulders over which we have to climb while also trying to avoid their sharp protrusions that threaten to cut up our hands. The iron rungs that line the entire ascent make our pace excruciatingly slow as we each must clip and unclip from every single rung to prevent us from falling off the mountain.

I wish I could say I enjoy the hike. But I find my happy place in a hard challenge, not a terrifying one. And while the safety of being clipped in eliminates any real chance of death, it is nowhere near the definition of a fun time for me. It takes a lot of digging deep, a lot of sustained breaths, and a lot of trying not to focus on the fact that I will have to do this all over again on the way back down the mountain. The peaks that lead up to Triglav greet me at my personal edge and taunt repeatedly, "Are you sure that's all you've got?" And so I dig even deeper, breathe even harder, and climb.

Reaching the summit is worth all the effort. It always is. Not just for the beauty but also because the act of climbing a peak changes you by the time you reach its topmost point. I arrive just a bit traumatized but as an expanded and stronger version of who I was at the bottom of the mountain. My new friends and I laugh and take photos while we enjoy the still-flawless weather gracing the mountains around us. The way back, to my relief, is much easier. We even decide to forgo part of the trail to giddily slide bottom-first down a patch of glacial snow.

To my delight, the places I hike after that day on Triglav somehow continue to be more and more magnificent, with each vista ever more awe-inspiring. It's as if the glory of the Julian Alps is my reward for braving its highest summit. These mountains have definitively laid claim to my heart, and I know I'll forever remember their charm, their challenge, and their invitation to deepen my knowledge of who I am. But when my trip reaches its conclusion after five glorious days, I feel my learning and growth here are complete. Walking this internal and external journey through the Julian Alps, I have emerged better on the other side, and now it is time to leave magical Slovenia to return to the arms of my love (right after I conquer the Liechtenstein Way!).

LOGISTICS

Choosing a Route

There are hundreds of miles of trails in the Julian Alps, so choosing a route can be daunting. One option is to hike the entire Julian Alps Hiking Trail, which covers 186 miles, takes sixteen days to complete, and covers the most magnificent sections of the mountain range. If you do not want to hike the entire length, you can hike one or more of the sixteen sections, or stages.

Additionally, many guide companies offer itineraries for a hut-to-hut hike. You can google different options and either copy their suggested itineraries or contract with an agency to place your bookings and plan your route.

If you want to book the huts on your own, visit the website for the alpine Association of Slovenia.

I chose to hire Helia Travel to arrange my trip. They handled all the bookings and transfers and made the experience incredibly easy. You can learn more about their Julian Alps offerings on their website.

Getting to the Trailhead

All international flights arrive in Ljubljana. From there, you can take a two-hour bus ride to Lake Bohinj, located at the foot of the Julian Alps. From Lake Bohinj, there are two options to get into the Alps: walk from the lake straight up the mountainside or take a gondola into the mountains.

Length and Difficulty

You can hike as long as you'd like in the Julian Alps. My itinerary from Helia Travel was five days of hiking and thirty-seven miles. The terrain is difficult but not technical outside of the optional Triglav summit. Since I finished a day early (I like to hike fast!), I added a day hike to Vogel Mountain from Lake Bohinj, which was phenomenal.

Accommodations

Camping is not allowed in the Julian Alps, so all overnight hikers must stay in the mountain huts. The huts are simple but have restaurants and most basic amenities. Staying at the huts is an excellent opportunity to meet hikers from around the world.

Best Time to Hike

The best time to hike in the Julian Alps is between April and October.

Pro Tips

Get ready for some of the most resplendent hiking you have ever seen! The Julian Alps are spectacular.

Those who have a fear of heights might want to skip summiting Triglav, but if you choose to hike to the summit, I recommend doing some preliminary research on hiking the *via ferrata* before you go. Also, be sure to arrange to rent safety equipment through your hut before you arrive and start your hike at daybreak to catch the sunrise.

If your schedule allows, I highly recommend visiting Lake Bled and taking a ride on a wooden boat to its stunning island church.

Also, eat a ton of local sauerkraut. It is simply delicious.

BOOKS

The Julian Alps of Slovenia: Mountain Walks and Short Treks by Justi Carey and Roy Clark (Cicerone Press Limited).

LOCAL LANGUAGE: SLOVENE

Thank you: Hvala (hu-WAH-lah)
Please: Prosím (PRO-seem)
I'm sorry: Oprostite (oh-PRO-STEE-ta)

REGIONAL RECIPE

Never was a meal served without the option of delicious sauerkraut. It became my favorite staple on trail. This is a recipe for a traditional Slovenian stew where sauerkraut plays a star role.

SAUERKRAUT AND BEAN STEW

(Slovenian Jota)

Serves 4–6

INGREDIENTS

2 medium potatoes, peeled and cut into 1-inch pieces

2 tbsp olive oil

1 large onion, diced

4 garlic cloves, minced

2 bay leaves

2 tbsp tomato paste

1 tbsp smoked paprika

2 ½ cups of sauerkraut, rinsed

4 cups vegetable broth or water

2 (15.5 oz) cans of borlotti beans, drained and rinsed (you can substitute pinto or kidney beans)

salt and pepper to taste

agave to taste

DIRECTIONS

1. Place potatoes in a small pot and cover with cold water so the potatoes are submerged by an inch. Bring water to a boil on high heat, then reduce to low or medium and cover the pan with a lid. Potatoes should cook in the water for 10–15 minutes.

2. While potatoes are cooking, add olive oil to a large pot and heat on medium heat. Add onions and cook until translucent, about 5 minutes.

3. Add garlic and sauté another 1–2 minutes.

4. Add bay leaves, tomato paste, smoked paprika, sauerkraut, and 2 cups of water or vegetable stock. Mix well and bring to a simmer.

5. Check that potatoes are cooked by piercing with a knife. If they're soft, drain water and mash potatoes with a fork. Then add them to the large pot with another 2 cups of water or broth and mix well.

6. Let broth simmer for 15 minutes with the lid ajar to retain the liquid.

7. Add beans and stir and simmer for a further 20 minutes.

8. Grind some pepper to taste and add salt if needed. For a sweeter flavor, add tbsp of agave. Remove the bay leaves and serve.

The Liechtenstein Way

July 2019

DIFFICULTY: Easy | **LENGTH: 46 miles (74 km)** | **ELEVATION GAIN: 7,162 feet (2,183 m)** | **DURATION: 3 days**

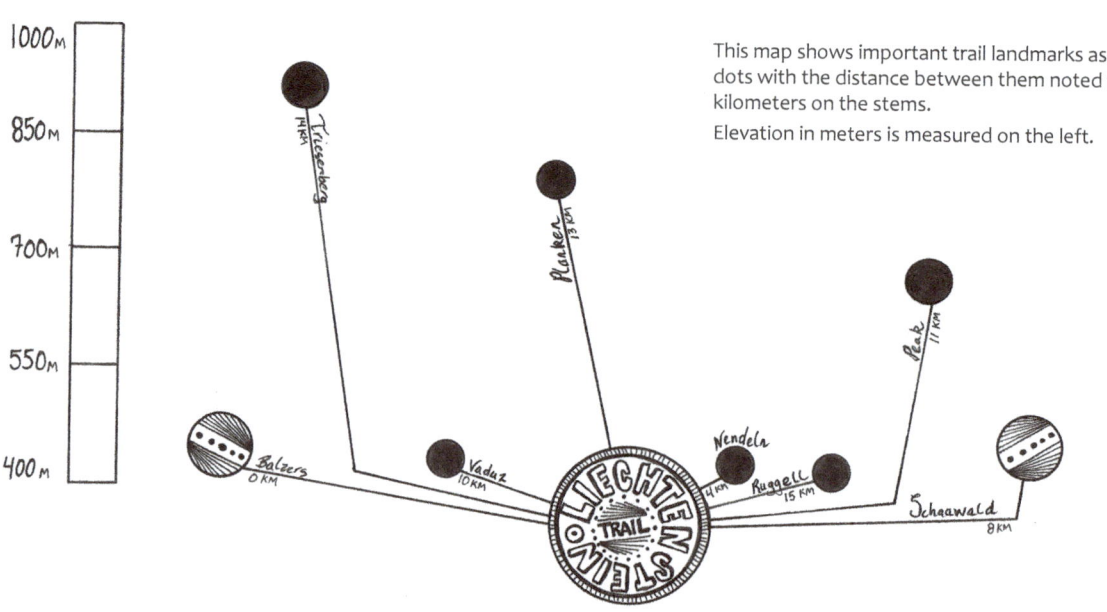

This map shows important trail landmarks as dots with the distance between them noted in kilometers on the stems.
Elevation in meters is measured on the left.

Walk as if you are kissing the Earth with your feet.

—THICH NHAT HAHN

 LESSON... **Accept the gift you're given.**

I'll be the first to admit it: I was seduced by an article in *National Geographic*. And it wasn't the first time either. In fact, many of my hikes have been inspired by the glossy pictures in magazines like *Nat Geo*. While friends are endlessly scrolling social media, I'm obsessively searching for what the experts on all things travel deem the most scenic hikes in the world.

And up to this point, *National Geographic* had not let me down.

Their article about the Liechtenstein Way painted a picture of a Camino-like experience: walking the length of an entire country (in only three days!) and being rewarded with gorgeous castles, epic mountains, and historic churches along the way. Completing this hike also came with bragging rights for having hiked the length of the sixth-smallest country in the world.

I was all in.

The Liechtenstein Way was created to celebrate the country's 300th anniversary, and I could tell a lot of energy, funds, and PR resources had been put into the endeavor. A corresponding app provides historical background about the sites along the trail. Shops in larger towns offer hats and bags and stickers so you can show off that you've completed the challenge. And there are signs plastered everywhere pointing the way.

As a country, Liechtenstein is most famous for being a tax haven and for its Gutenberg Castle, an imposing medieval structure that overlooks the semi-picturesque town of Vaduz. Upon arriving, I quickly drop my luggage at my delightfully stylish hotel and begin to hike up to the castle grounds.

The castle is simply stunning. Though privately owned and inaccessible on the inside, the outside is truly impressive. In my opinion, it's the epitome of what

a castle should be—immaculately preserved and a bit spooky, with a touch of regal energy mixed in. I love it. If this castle is a sign of what's to come, I think, a few great days lie ahead.

This positive forecast is in direct contrast to the gloomy outlook offered by my dear friend Sabine, who is originally from Switzerland. Before I flew to Europe, I was excitedly chatting with her about my upcoming Liechtenstein adventure, but the more I shared, the more Sabine looked confused.

"Liechtenstein??" she asked, aghast. "Are you sure you want to go there? There's only one main road. It's just a tax haven. Ugly. Not interesting. You should go to Switzerland instead."

But I pulled out my phone and showed her photos of castles and pristine forests and told her that she was mistaken, that it was going to be a gorgeous walk, that this trail would take me through all of the spectacular areas she'd simply not seen during her time there. She looked unimpressed. "Switzerland," she repeated. "That's where you should go."

Despite Sabine's warning, I hold fast to the belief that this trip is the right choice for me and that the castle is a harbinger of the jaw-dropping countryside waiting to be explored. But the next day as I board the local bus to the beginning of the trail, I start to question my decision. Looking around, I note that the scenery is pretty plain. Sure, there are gorgeous mountains on either side of the towns we pass through, but the actual countryside where I'll be trekking is just one long road stretching blandly between the beauty. Sabine was right—Switzerland is where the gorgeous hiking is. *Nat Geo* had led me astray.

The Liechtenstein Way starts at the Liechtenstein-Austria border where a small sign indicates that you are at the beginning of the trail. I unceremoniously exit the bus and begin to walk. Unlike most hikes I've completed where there's typically a crowd of people (or at least a few) on the trail, I find myself completely alone. Usually this solitude is something I cherish, but here I fear it portends an underwhelming experience. The only things keeping me company are the strategically placed information boards and all the cows. So many cows! I quickly become quite adept at navigating cow patties, a skill I didn't particularly want to hone.

When not entertaining myself with cattle counting, I meander through towns that honestly lack any real beauty or originality. I do hike past some abandoned castles, which are a highlight to be sure, but there are only a few along the entire path. I do appreciate seeing the old Bavarian-style buildings that served as refuge for the homeless during medieval times and for Jews during World War II. And there are at least a few lovely churches, which provide picnic benches and shade, but these few points of interest are about all the enjoyment this trail offers. Even the stretches that take me away from the towns and into the forest are underwhelming. Sadly, so many trees have been cut down and piled for lumber that the woods look more like a timber graveyard than a scenic mountain woodland.

And then there's the traffic noise.

Sabine was correct. There's one major road that runs through the length of this country. It sits low in the basin between two mountain ranges that create a type of sound barrier. The noise from Liechtenstein's main road is reflected by the mountains and amplified back through the valley. This means that all I hear, day in and day out, is the heightened sound of screeching tires and honking horns. No matter how high I climb or the seemingly sheltered areas I reach, I can't escape this invasive and persistent unpleasantness.

On all hikes, I try to find something to be grateful for, even when the going gets exceedingly difficult. And I do have a few moments of success with this gratitude practice in Liechtenstein. I see an occasional pretty house. I eat a picnic in a gorgeous church garden. I spot a rolling meadow brimming with wildflowers. And there's a beautiful winery in the town of Vaduz that also distills some of the best whiskey I have ever tasted in all my travels. Finding that whiskey almost makes the rest of the trip worth it.

Almost.

●●●●

When I arrive at the end of the Liechtenstein Way, it is as underwhelming as most of the trail. There is no flag or plaque congratulating me for a job well done. No statue to symbolize the hike's completion. Just a government checkpoint indicating the end of Liechtenstein and the beginning of Switzerland, where I probably should have been all along.

As I make my way back to the hotel in Vaduz, sunburned, tired, and craving respite from the street noise that has filled my ears for three days, I try to reflect on possible lessons from my time here. First, I vow I'll never again be lured to a destination by pretty pictures or a fetching story in a travel magazine alone (I'm going to need some further evidence of the locale's merit!). Second, I remind myself to always prioritize the experience of being somewhere truly stunning and unique over earning bragging rights for, say, hiking through an entire country. And third, I realize that maybe it's time to give up trying to snag as many passport stamps as I can. Maybe I am being called to transition from quantity to quality, and this hike helped me grow into a more discerning adventurer. Perhaps that's why I was meant to come to Liechtenstein after all.

LOGISTICS

Choosing a Route

The Liechtenstein Way is a single trail that runs through the entire country. It's well marked and easy to follow.

Getting to the Trailhead

The closest international airport to Liechtenstein is in Zurich, Switzerland. From the airport, you can take a two-hour train ride to Buchs, Switzerland, where you can hail a taxi to Vaduz. From Vaduz, take a local bus to the start of the trail located in the town of Balzers at the Liechtenstein-Austria border.

Length and Difficulty

The trail is forty-six miles long and mostly flat with a few short climbs.

Accommodations

There are hotels to stay in along the trail. Alternatively, it's possible to stay at the same hotel in Vaduz and take buses to and from different parts of the trail each day. Camping is not an option along the trail.

Best Time to Hike

The best time to walk this trail is between April and October.

Pro Tips

Make sure to download the Liechtenstein Way app before you begin your hike. The app not only has a good interactive map but also provides historical information about the sites along the trail.

I recommend spending some time at Princely Wine Cellars outside of Vaduz. Their wines are lovely and their whiskey outstanding. Also, the Liechtenstein Postal Museum makes for a sweet afternoon visit.

And make sure to get your passport stamped at the visitor's center in Vaduz!

BOOKS

Liechtenstein Travel Guide: Tourism by Jesse Russell (independently published).

LOCAL LANGUAGE: GERMAN

Thank you: Vielen dank (FEEL-in dah-nk)
Please: Bitte (BIT-ah)
I'm sorry: Es tut mir leid (es TOOT me-er light)

REGIONAL RECIPE

This is not a recipe that I tried on trail since a vegan version was not available, but *ribel* is considered one of the four main traditional dishes of Liechtenstein. Here's a vegan version of the breakfast classic.

RIBEL

Serves 4

INGREDIENTS

1⅛ cups plant-based milk

1⅛ cups water

1 tsp salt

2 ½ cups cornmeal (or polenta)

1–2 tbsp vegan butter

sugar for sprinkling

½ cup fruit compote

DIRECTIONS

1. Put milk, water, salt, and 1 tsp of vegan butter in a pan and bring to a boil.

2. Add cornmeal and stir until all the liquid is absorbed. Remove the pan from heat and let it stand, covered, for about 15 minutes.

3. Remove the lid and return the pan to high heat, cooking mixture until it turns very crumbly, about 5 minutes. You can gradually add in more butter (or a splash of milk, if needed) as it continues to cook.

4. Reduce heat to medium, stirring mixture frequently. Let it stand for a minute from time to time until all the liquid is absorbed.

5. Sprinkle with sugar and serve with coffee and fruit compote.

Appalachian Trail Across the Great Smoky Mountains

November 2020

DIFFICULTY: Strenuous | LENGTH: **72 miles (116 km)** | ELEVATION GAIN: **21,600 feet (6,584 m)** | DURATION: **4–7 days**

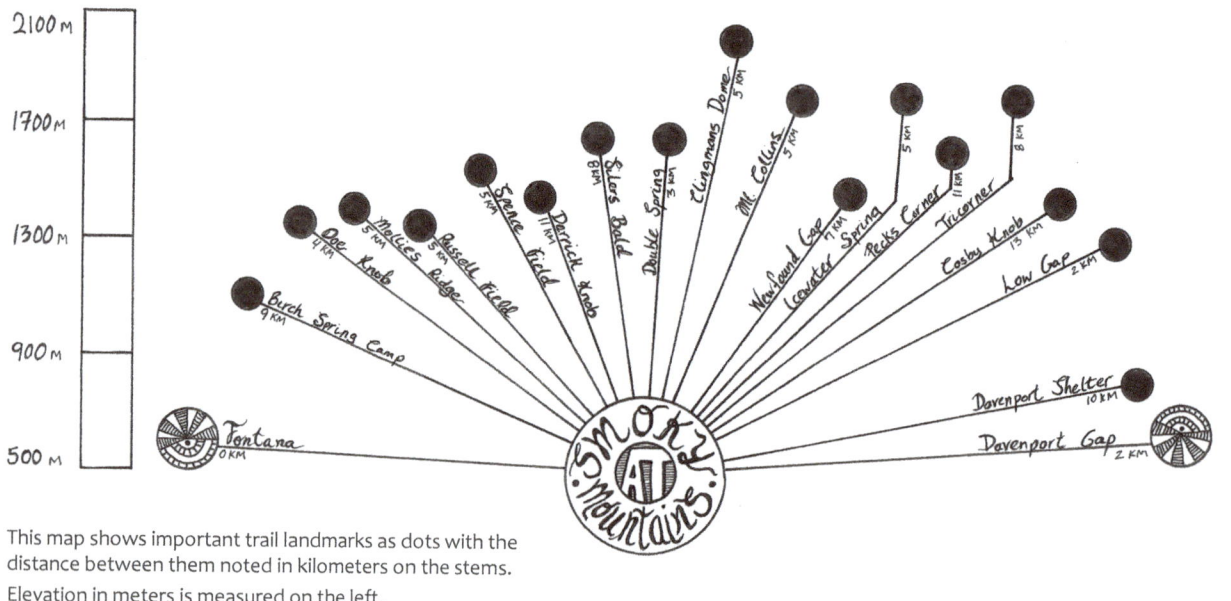

This map shows important trail landmarks as dots with the distance between them noted in kilometers on the stems. Elevation in meters is measured on the left.

Happiness is the struggle towards a summit and, when it is attained, it is happiness to glimpse new summits on the other side.

—FRIDTJOF NANSEN

●●●●● LESSON... **Ease over ego.** ●●●●●

Emily is significantly ahead of me. I can see her signature colors (black hiking clothes and a blue backpack) moving farther away as she seems to effortlessly climb the steep ascent. With each additional foot of distance between us, I feel my spirit dampen a little. Emily, my Asheville neighbor and hometown hiking partner, is usually just a touch slower than I am, which I appreciate, because outside of hiking, she's athletically superior to me in every way. Being just the slightest bit faster as a hiker makes me feel better when I struggle at everything else at which Emily excels, such as running, surfing, or mountain biking (or even owning a bike, for that matter).

But today I know I will not be passing Emily on trail. Today my body is seriously struggling in ways I'm not used to. Today I am being forced to face a fear that I was desperately hoping to avoid.

One of my lungs is not okay.

In my work as an alternative healer, I often make the rounds to the varied metaphysical practitioners in my town for my own healing. I'm lured in by their promises to clear my chakras, cleanse my childhood traumas, and remove any remnants of negative energy from past lives. To achieve these ambitious goals, they use a variety of methods, including energy work, acupuncture, administering plant medicines, or skillfully sounding gongs and chimes in my presence.

And I love all of it! The feeling of joyousness that comes after treatments, the sense of having an energetic reset, the way my life becomes easier the more I clear that which does not serve me. Alternative healing truly is my life raft in the world, and my "go-to" when things are not right in my body or in my heart.

In September of 2020, Matt and I decided to take the next step and married on a gorgeous mountaintop in Asheville. The weather was perfect, the ceremony delightful, and though the celebration was small and socially distanced, it was still filled to the brim with joy. Sadly, only a week later, I developed a mysterious non-COVID respiratory virus that left me bedridden for sixteen painfully boring days. Knowing how beneficial I had found acupuncture in the past, I did not hesitate to reach out to my practitioner for a session. I assured her that two negative COVID tests and sixteen days of a "just in case" quarantine rendered me safe, and she squeezed me in for an appointment the next day.

Convinced that my illness was in fact COVID, she began to place needles around my chest and torso to clear the virus from my lungs. For some reason, the needles hurt more than usual, especially one particular needle placed directly under my right breast. When I told her how uncomfortable it felt, she assured me that it was merely the power of the treatment fighting the COVID, and though it was painful, as soon as she removed the needles, I would feel amazing.

Truthfully, I barely made it through the session. The pain from that one needle was almost unbearable (and I have quite the pain tolerance). The more I told her that something was wrong, the more she claimed to be receiving guidance from "above" to keep pushing that needle in farther. And farther and farther in it went.

When she did finally take the needles out, I could barely move. I felt dizzy and nauseated and slightly traumatized. Though I probably shouldn't have driven home, I was desperate to get back to Matt and my bed. I immediately developed a terrible cough that shook my entire body for the next eight hours. Something was very, very wrong. When I called the acupuncturist to ask her what I should do, she assured me that my physical symptoms were a result of old emotional trauma, and if I just journaled about my feelings, I would lift myself out of pain.

Hearing that from her really pissed me off.

The following morning, I went to urgent care. The admitting doctor had a hypothesis that seemed completely unfathomable to me. But when the X-ray came back, it confirmed the worst.

My acupuncturist had partially collapsed my lung.

There are two potential outcomes after a nonfatal pneumothorax: the best-case scenario is that the lung inflates on its own in a couple of weeks; the worst case is that a tube must be inserted to refill the collapsed lung. Fortunately, my lung followed its own healing path, and I was able to avoid hospitalization. Unfortunately, Matt and I had to postpone our honeymoon to Alaska since flying with a punctured lung is a pretty clear trajectory to an early demise. Had I followed my acupuncturist's suggestion of simply journaling about my feelings and still traveled as planned, I would most likely not be writing this today.

Hiking was out of the question for weeks following the pneumothorax. And so I waited impatiently, hoping that I would heal enough to soon return to the trail, though fearing that the injury might render me "trail-less" for the rest of my life.

I have a really bad habit of catastrophizing when injured.

Thankfully, three weeks later, an X-ray showed that my lung had reinflated, and the doctor cleared me to go back to normal exercise. The timing was perfect because it meant that Emily and I could move forward with our plan to fulfill one of our many backpacking bucket-list goals—to through-hike the Smoky Mountains on the Appalachian Trail (AT).

For the duration of the high season on the AT, which lasts from sometime in March through September, my friends and I avoid the AT and nearby trails like the plague since they are consistently overrun with far too many people. The campsites feel like overbooked vacation destinations, and any sense of solitude or tranquility is completely lost during that time.

But November! Now that's a great month to be on the AT. Barely anyone is on trail, the sleeping huts are close to empty, and there's so much quiet. Granted, you never know what type of weather you might encounter, but where the lung gods had been wrathful with me that fall, the weather gods chose to bless us that November with sun and clear skies almost every day— something pretty rare in a mountain range named after heavy clouds.

Even without my recent injury, I know this hike will be a tough one. The AT through the Smoky Mountains can only be described as an unrelenting trek. It traverses the highest spine of the range, which claims multiple peaks above 6,000 feet, and rarely comes below 5,000 feet after the first huge ascent. When I'm up that high, I like to think that I've entered the playground of the gods—it feels so mystical at those elevations. I find it motivating to envision this reward as I labor upwards, imagining that the payoff for my mortal exertion will be a high-elevation encounter with the divine.

But just like the protagonist of any Greek tale, I have my own inner demons to conquer on this hike. My body feels compromised. As I watch Emily climb higher and higher, I can barely keep her in view. My heart rate is alarmingly elevated. My breathing is labored. I'm scared I might have to call it and return home.

By lunchtime, I realize that I need to have a serious conversation with myself. I sit down on the trail's edge to assess what is happening to me. I recognize that I'm in the throes of an ego-versus-reality battle, and no one is winning. It's so hard for me to accept not being in good physical condition and to have to go slow. I have no idea where this hang-up comes from, but it is real. Still, I know that if I try to push myself the way I usually do, I will not be able to continue, and that will really break my heart.

So I make a deal with myself. I decide that I will do my best to go as slow as needed so my heart rate does not become elevated (since every time I start to breathe heavily, my lung aches). And if my heart rate does increase, I will take breaks to bring it down. Doing this might mean a slower hike but also guarantees a greater likelihood of actually completing the trail in the end.

When I finally get to camp later that night, Emily (who is one of the most talented body workers I know) tells me that she believes this hike is good spring training for my injured lung. By showing my lung what I expect from it, I am breaking through scar tissue, as well as programming my brain to instruct my lung to return to its normal state. This framework is really helpful: it pulls me out of my fear and brings me back to a mentality focused on hope and healing.

And so Emily and I continue our AT hike. Being the overachievers that we are, we decide to cut the hiking time short and conquer the seventy-two miles in four days instead of five (still being cognizant of my reduced lung capacity, of course). My motivation: I want to be home in time for vegan pizza on Sunday night. The hiking doesn't get any easier (there are almost no switchbacks on the AT in the Smokies—just a trail that goes directly up the tallest part of every mountain), but wow, the scenery is beautiful. Every day presents postcard-perfect images of a sea of seemingly endless mountains.

Our second night, we camp three miles from the summit of Clingmans Dome (which might soon be renamed Kuwahi, its original Cherokee name as endorsed by the Eastern Band of Cherokee Indians). I have summited the mountain twice before but was always disappointed by a view obstructed by thick cloud cover. Never before had this mountaintop graced me with the magnificence she claimed.

The morning of our Clingmans summit, we wake at 5:00 a.m. to get a head start on a long day and quietly put together our packs so as not to disturb the other campers at our site. It is not until we are hiking by the light of our headlamps that we realize we might reach the summit in time for sunrise. Hiking in the dark feels magical to me. All you see is your foot placement directly ahead of you, highlighted by the beam of your headlamp. And there's a profound predawn quiet. With the forest creatures still mostly asleep, nighttime is when the mountains feel at rest as well.

I find the climb slow and laborious, and my spirit is lifted only by the fact that the darkness hides our view of the intimidating ascent ahead. Though I usually love hiking solo, I am so grateful to navigate the dark woods with Emily by my side. Together, we distract each other from the predawn spookiness and the strain of our intense exertion with stories about our lives, our thoughts about the world, and our dreams about future hikes yet to be conquered. And sometimes we just complain to each other. When suffering through a really hard uphill slog, it always helps to know someone else is suffering with you.

About halfway up Clingmans, we come upon a small open field and turn off our headlamps to take in the expanse of star-filled sky. It feels as if some divine being has thrown a handful of glitter against a black backdrop and named it "illumination." We are silent as we stand under the stars, acknowledging the profound privilege of being able to bask in their undiluted astronomical light. That moment of quietly absorbing starlight is all we need to fuel our souls for the last mile of uphill standing between us and the highest point in the Smoky Mountains.

After reaching the crest, we climb the odd, spaceship-shaped, man-made viewing platform on the mountain's summit as the faintest strip of searing red pierces the blackness of the night sky to the east. We feel energized standing next to other observers who had driven up the mountain (to experience what it took us thirty-five miles of hard hiking to achieve). Taking out our camp stoves, we quickly boil water to hydrate our oatmeal and coffee. Breakfast tastes especially delicious that day.

Little by little, the reds in the sky turn to orange, then to yellow, setting the stage for the rising of the sun. Ever so slowly, she begins to show her perfect circular luminosity. Having completed her time on the other side of the world, she now joins us to welcome the splendor of this new day.

Of all the photos Emily and I have taken on trail during the last few years, the one from the morning on Clingmans continues to be my favorite. To me, it represents what it means to overcome varied and formidable adversities to see the sunrise once again. That image of us, huddled together holding hot beverages with ridiculous grins on our faces, is the ultimate tribute to why I continue to put that pack on my back and endure physical pain, bug bites, scary summit traverses, sleepless nights, and countless other challenges. It's because those singular moments of transcendence are, for me, worth far more than what it costs to achieve them.

On the last day of our hike, we arrive at our final push: Mount Cammerer, elevation 4,928 feet. Though it's hard for me to imagine finding the strength to make it up this one final ascent, I know that the only way I'll be able to get to the car and my soon-to-be-ordered pizza is by willing myself over this final peak. Needing to recharge both physically and mentally before this final effort, I find a semi-flat rock where I can sit and slowly eat a granola bar, aware that as soon as I take my last bite, I'll have to start the climb.

As I am putting my backpack on after my snack, I hear Emily catching up to me. Having hiked separately all morning, we exchange quick observations about our trail time, such as "The wind was crazy! I thought this tree was going to be ripped from its roots!" and "Were you scared of being blown off the mountain?" before we begin our slow ascent. My muscles are screaming in pain, but I have no choice. There is only one possible direction that will bring me home.

As soon as we begin the climb, Emily asks me if I am aware that there is a grasshopper on my leg. I look down to see the most interesting-looking grasshopper I've ever come across. Instead of green, its body is a mosaic of beautiful browns, at least three inches long, and about the thickness of a hummingbird. I gently try to shake it off, but it refuses to budge. When I look down, the grasshopper seems to squarely return my gaze. One final shake, and I give up, deciding instead to offer this magnificent insect a ride up the mountainside.

For almost thirty minutes, my grasshopper friend holds its place. And instead of wanting it off of me, I find real comfort in its presence. It's as if this grasshopper is my Smoky Mountain spirit animal, there to help me overcome the final challenge ahead.

About halfway up Mount Cammerer, I look down to notice that my newfound friend has moved on to its next adventure. Perhaps I'd taken it to the place it was seeking all along. Even without it there, I carry its energy all the way to the summit and take each step with a little more resolve. And the magic of the morning continues even after my little friend's departure. Coming around a curve, I'm greeted with multiple rainbows and, after that, a spectacular view of a majestic pass over lush green mountains, which seem to billow like verdant clouds across the landscape below.

It has now been just over a year since I stood proudly on that mountaintop, taking in the magnificent breadth of one of the most glorious mountain ranges in the United States. Since then, my lung has completely healed, and though I have faced a few other physical hurdles in the interim, I once again feel strong on trail. And while I've continued to seek out majestic places and challenging climbs, from time to time, I do still need an emotional boost to push me onward. During these tough moments when I struggle to find my motivation, I sometimes imagine that determined grasshopper once again hitching a ride and cheering me on. Often, it's just the little push I need to continue uphill.

LOGISTICS

Choosing a Route

The Appalachian Trail is a well-blazed route through the Smoky Mountains.

Getting to the Trailhead

This hike is point-to-point, meaning that you either have to arrange a shuttle or leave a car at each trailhead. The trail can be hiked in either direction, though hiking northbound is more typical. From that direction, the AT enters the park from the south at Fontana Dam, where there's ample parking. You'll walk across a bridge that spans the dam to continue the trail. In the northeast, the trail exits the park at Davenport Gap.

I suggest leaving a car at whichever location will be your endpoint and arranging a shuttle to bring you to the beginning of your hike.

If you need to set up a shuttle ride, a company I've used in the past is Carolina Bound Adventures.

Length and Difficulty

Make no mistake, the AT through the Smokies is a tough hike. You'll gain a total of 21,600 feet over almost seventy-two miles. On average, it takes seven days to complete but can be done in as few as four.

Accommodations

AT shelters and campsites are located along the route and need to be reserved in advance. The shelters contain wooden platforms where you can set up a sleeping bag. While it's recommended that hikers stay in the shelters to minimize the impact on the land, it's also a good idea to bring a tent in case the shelters are full.

Best Time to Hike

Most people that hike the AT northbound will complete the Smokies section sometime between April and the end of May. Therefore, I'd recommend hiking the Smokies between June and November. The later in the season, the more solitude you'll find on trail.

Pro Tips

The Smoky Mountains are famous for their many black bears. Be sure to make noise every time you come around a blind curve so you don't startle a furry resident around the bend. I love the poem about bear encounters that warns "if it's brown, lie down; if it's black, fight back." This is an oversimplification, but in general, if you see a black bear, make yourself big and loud; they're generally skittish and will in all likelihood just run away. If attacked by a black bear, fight back; do not play dead. And it's always a good idea to carry bear spray. Still, rest assured that bear attacks are incredibly rare! Every time I've seen a bear in the Smokies, it has quickly darted away from me.

Also, before you go, download the FarOut Guides app and purchase the part with information about the Smokies section of the AT. It's an amazing resource for elevation information, water sources, and campsites.

BOOKS

Becoming Odyssa: Adventures on the Appalachian Trail by Jennifer Pharr Davis (Beaufort Books).

Hiking: Great Smoky Mountains National Park by Kevin Adams (Falcon Guides).

REGIONAL RECIPE

There's a pickled relish famous in Appalachia that's often served as an accompaniment to beans and cornbread. Perfectly balanced between sweet and savory, chow chow definitely adds a unique flavor to any meal.

CHOW CHOW RELISH

Serves 8–10

INGREDIENTS

3 cups diced bell pepper

2 cups grated cabbage

2 cups diced onion

2 cups diced green tomato

1 jalapeño pepper, minced

1 tbsp salt

1 tsp mustard seeds

½ tsp celery seeds

⅔ cup sugar

¼ cup apple cider vinegar

½ tsp crushed red pepper flakes

½ tsp ground mustard

¼ tsp ginger

¼ tsp turmeric

DIRECTIONS

1. In a large bowl, combine bell peppers, cabbage, onions, green tomatoes, jalapeño, and salt (tip: shredding the vegetables in a food processor will cut down on cooking time). Cover with plastic wrap and refrigerate overnight.

2. In the morning, drain liquid from vegetable mixture.

3. In a large pot, toast mustard seeds and celery seeds until they are fragrant and begin to pop, about 2–3 minutes.

4. Add sugar, apple cider vinegar, and 1 cup of water to the toasted seeds and stir until sugar is dissolved.

5. Add drained vegetable mixture, along with the crushed red pepper flakes, mustard powder, turmeric, and ginger and bring to a boil.

6. Reduce the heat to a simmer and stir occasionally, leaving the pot uncovered. Simmer until the mixture is thick, about 1 hour.

7. Remove from heat and let cool. Serve as a condiment on your favorite vegan hot dog or mix with some vegan cream cheese for an amazing dip! Chow chow will stay fresh for about a week in the fridge in an airtight container.

Shar Mountains

June 2021

DIFFICULTY: Strenuous | LENGTH: **41 miles (66 km)** | ELEVATION GAIN: **19,584 feet (5,969 m)** | DURATION: **5 days**

Different peaks along the trail in North Macedonia and their corresponding height in meters.

Until you step into the unknown,
you don't know what you are made of.

—ROY T. BENNETT

●○●● LESSON... Find your reference point. ●●●●

It's the Sunday before I'm supposed to leave for North Macedonia, and honestly, I'm not doing very well. In fact, things are quite bad. I have left the realm of rational thought and find myself in a dramatic downward emotional spiral. I've completely succumbed to panic and despair.

I open my laptop and start the painful process of canceling my trip. I email the tour group to let them know I can't complete the itinerary due to injury. I cancel my starting and ending hotels in Skopje and Boston. And then I just sit and cry. Matt is at a loss as to how to console me. He places one of his long arms around my shoulders and quietly holds space as I fall apart.

Something is very wrong with my body. And no doctor or healer can figure out the cause of my shooting leg pain and buckling knees. In fact, the more confused professionals I see, the more desperate I become for a diagnosis. But while each has a different idea about what is happening to my legs, no one can actually provide any answers. I leave each appointment more scared than when I went in.

I am terrified I'll never hike again.

So here's what happened. Three months earlier, I went to see a spinal doctor to help me with some chronic lower-back pain. During our initial consultation, he suggested a series of steroid shots to ease the inflammation in my back. The possibility of a quick fix for a long-term issue was more than enticing, and I enthusiastically made an appointment for the invasive procedure.

What I now understand is that while administering the steroid shot, the doctor mistakenly pierced a nerve next to my spine. Consequently, this nerve stopped sending the signals that tell my quads what to do, and in turn, my quads stopped doing their job of holding my knees in place. When both knees buckled while I was on a run the week after the shot, causing serious and continuous pain, I panicked.

So back to the same doctor I went, and this time he prescribed oral steroids, which produced an allergic reaction. For three weeks, waves of fire ran down the front of my legs, and my knees repeatedly gave out, but no one could figure out why. I was told I needed yet more MRIs...nerve blockers...prescription-strength anti-inflammatories.... But emotionally, I just couldn't continue to trust Western medicine. Too much harm had already been done.

When I was still suffering symptoms the week before my North Macedonian adventure, I wasn't sure I'd be able to go. My body still hurt, and I couldn't imagine hiking in so much pain. Also, I wasn't sure it was a good idea to be so far from home in such bad shape.

My sadness was not specifically about the regret of not seeing North Macedonia. I had chosen this country a few days after getting my first COVID vaccine when my urge to travel finally began to stir after a year of hibernation. Getting my shots made me feel safe enough to board a plane and reclaim my travel spirit. As a destination, North Macedonia filled the criteria of (1) being open to Americans, (2) having mountains, and (3) being someplace I had not yet been.

Rather, canceling this trip felt symbolically like canceling my entire future of hiking adventures around the world. I know this sounds dramatic, but I was really freaked out at the time. Holding on to the hope of going to North Macedonia represented holding on to the belief that I would one day heal from what no one yet understood. My heart needed this trip as a sign that I was once again on the path toward the life I had previously known and cherished.

My feelings of sadness were all-consuming that Sunday evening, but when I woke Monday morning to begin my daily meditation, something wonderful and profound happened.

For some reason, I started to think about wine.

I do like a great glass of wine and have a big, bold red with dinner a few times a week (during the pandemic, that number was perhaps a bit higher…). Wine tasting in foreign countries is something I quite enjoy. I already knew North Macedonia boasted a delightful wine region, and I thought, If I can't hike, I can still drink.

Fortunately, the Wednesday before I was to leave, something in my body also shifted. While taking a hot shower after an easy, flat hike, my most intense nerve pain largely disappeared. Not all of it, but the worst of it. I think the hot water helped ease the inflammation in my spine, which had been compressing the nerve. I was scared to trust this relief would last, but I did start to feel just the slightest glimmer of hope. My legs were not fully recovered, but they were not the hot mess they had been. Perhaps, I considered, I actually have a chance of walking trails in North Macedonia after all.

Sometimes when I ponder a life without hiking, I lose sight of the complex components that make me who I am outside of my time on trail. For instance, I love art. I enjoy volunteering internationally. Also, going on spiritual retreats has become an integral part of my internal growth. And even after everywhere I've traveled, a gorgeous castle or cathedral still amazes me. But nonetheless, I sometimes forget that I'm more than a pair of trail runners and a good backpack. So for me, going to North Macedonia, even with injured knees, was actually a declaration of self-love. Even if I could not hike, I could still reclaim parts of me that for too long had been waiting in the wings while my hiking self took center stage.

And so I board the plane to North Macedonia without knowing what my trip will actually look like. But whether I see mountains or cities, winding trails or elegant wineries, I feel ready to create an adventure that will feed my soul.

As the plane begins its final descent after fourteen hours of travel, I look out the window to take in the landscape of this new-to-me country. There are mountains as far as I can see. Snow-peaked spires seemingly soar to just below the belly of the plane, and their mere presence brings me such profound happiness. If I can't hike them, at least I can be surrounded by their beauty.

I spend my first night in the capital city of Skopje, walking its winding streets and exploring the town square before getting lost in its ancient marketplace. Skopje is filled with magnificent statues that celebrate everyone from Alexander the Great to the noteworthy women who have shaped the country's history. The city also lays claim to being the home of Mother Teresa, and I make a pilgrimage to her house the following day. Seeing her handwritten documents and learning more about her selfless commitment to the most vulnerable among us puts my minor health challenge into serious perspective.

The day before the first hike on my itinerary, I feel a sense of fragmentation: I vacillate between thinking I can do it and obsessing about the weird pattern of pain still present in my legs. I wake at 4:00 a.m. with that familiar panic rising in my chest. But this time, instead of succumbing to it, I send my fear deep breaths and work to bring calm to all the parts inside of me (emotional and physical) that are aflame.

A few hours later, I am on trail. The first two-mile stretch is practically vertical. And though I feel some leg discomfort, it's not worsened by the hike. In fact, that initial uphill makes my knees feel almost normal, as if they've recovered their muscle memory and now know what they need to do.

I happily continue to climb.

Eventually, the view of the ski-slope machinery transforms into pristine alpine splendor. Wildflowers are just beginning to bloom among the rocky outcrops and in grassy meadows, and there's a crispness in the air and a soothing silence only occasionally interrupted by the sounds of birds or sheep or dogs. Hypervigilant, I keep checking in with my knees, but they seem to have settled into a sweet painlessness. I sometimes feel a twinge of discomfort here, a hint of tension there. But overall, my mind and body are more in sync than I imagined possible.

I ascend three peaks this first day, overcoming 20 percent inclines, navigating snowfields, enduring a few spectacular falls, and enjoying one unintentional butt slide down a particularly challenging descent. And all this time, my body feels like it is coming home. Perhaps what my legs needed all along was simply an adventure, some mountain air, and time on trail.

I do really well on the hike until my last steep downhill, when my left knee calls it quits and begins throbbing. But I don't freak out or panic. I simply label it normal knee pain and trust that my body will heal, which I'm finally beginning to accept might be true.

The next day starts with a boring three-mile uphill slog through the forest. It feels underwhelming, but when I finally reach the Konak Hut in the Shar Mountains, the scenery changes dramatically. I emerge from the thick forest into the most glorious open mountain plain. Peaks topped with intricately patterned snow patches create a bowl around me, and the ground leading up to their high summits is adorned with newly blossoming spring flowers. After a quick rest and a cup of coffee, I begin the serious and quite challenging climb toward the ridge of Mount Ljuboten. Fortunately, and even maybe a bit magically, butterflies and dragonflies accompany

me along the trail, their fluttering wings and bright colors making my struggle up the mountain more enjoyable. Unfortunately, I've forgotten how the sense of distance can be a trickster at these elevations. Every time I think I'm close to reaching the summit, I see a taller peak behind it. And then a taller one behind that one.

This hike is seriously hard.

Eventually, the trail becomes a precariously thin, two-feet-wide path on a steep ridge, and I have to constantly navigate the dangers of sharp, loose rocks because one false step, and I will plummet thousands of feet to an untimely demise. I wonder how the staff at the local tourist agency thought that hiking up this treacherous mountain was a good idea. But nevertheless, I persevere.

When I think I simply do not have the strength or bravery to continue, I take a seriously deep breath and set an intention to just focus on each foot placement, and in this way, I proceed. At one point, I loudly scream, "I AM OUT OF MY COMFORT ZONE!" into the empty space around me, and this, for some reason, makes me feel a lot better.

Sometimes you just need to fall apart a little to go on.

When the actual peak comes into view, my jaw drops. She is craggy and mean and menacing, and though part of me wants to abandon this crazy endeavor and run back down to the comfort of my hut and a warm meal, I know myself well enough to admit that I will not turn away when the top is so near.

I push on.

And then, somehow, I'm on the summit of Mount Ljuboten, 8,200 feet in the air. The final hour of physical pain and emotional terror simply disappears as I take in the majesty of the mountains of North Macedonia to one side and alpine Kosovo to the other. It's all stunningly resplendent. I remind myself that descending a mountain is never as scary as the ascent, and after taking a few photos and deep breaths, I begin to make my way down.

A few hours later, my mountain hut comes into view, but instead of quickening my pace, I pause on the mountainside and take some time to just sit and breathe. After the intensity of the summit, the act of just being present in that field feels profoundly peaceful. For a full hour, I observe the mountains that form a semicircle around me. This one, covered in alpine forest. That one, sporting big ovals of cascading snow. Another one, covered in short grass and craggy rock. And that one, way in the distance, barren and harsh.

Even after six years of daily meditation practice, I rarely sink into the depth of mindfulness on my meditation chair that I can achieve on a sunny mountain ridge. I wish I could capture the unique essence of the peacefulness I feel in nature and preserve it to unpack when the stress of life becomes too much, when I need more than the respite of tuning into my own heart. I continue to sit, content to let time tick by until the draw of a hot shower and a cup of tea overpowers the serenity of my mountain perch. And so I begin my descent back to the hut and to the comforts waiting below.

It does not take long for me to fall in love with the couple who own the mountain villa where I'm staying tonight. Though neither speaks English, and my Macedonian does not extend past saying "thank you," we quickly fall into a sweet pattern of communicating with sweeping hand gestures and exaggerated facial expressions. Upon my arrival, I'm greeted with homemade brandy and warm congratulatory smiles (which I think are well deserved, if I do say so). Together, we sit at a robust carved wooden table as the husband, Victor, points to the framed photos of the surrounding mountains that decorate the walls of their home. He gestures to specific photos to show me where I will be hiking the next day. His excitement for what I have yet to see is as deep as my gratitude for what I have experienced so far.

After a decent night's sleep, I arrive at breakfast to find a large plate of tasty roasted vegetables. My delightful hosts are laughing and hugging me while they pour me my coffee. They are incredibly kind, and I know that these two people, who were strangers to me yesterday, will have a permanent place in my heart. As I leave the hut to continue my hike, a flurry of photos are taken, hugs given, more hugs given, and multiple kisses planted on both cheeks. I try to communicate my promise to visit again, and I really do mean it.

Encounters like these are one of the many reasons I adore hiking abroad. To me, the opportunity for cultural exchange is one of the most precious aspects of walking the mountains of another country. I love the chance to sample the local cuisine. To learn history from the perspective of those who lived it. To be reminded of how connection is so much bigger than verbal communication.

I begin my walk that day with much light and happiness in my heart.

The trail is perfect. It safely guides me around semi-precarious scree fields and more of the massive snow patches I've had to navigate throughout my trip thus far. At one point, I come across a gorgeous collection of rock boulders, and seeing them ignites a deep reservoir of bubbling joyousness inside me. It's a little unnerving how excited I get over a particularly majestic boulder. In my usual life at home, I do not get this worked up over rocks.

Throughout the day, I find myself completely alone in the landscape of the Shar Mountains as I walk silently among the endless expanse of green foothills and blue sky. I feel like I'm in the happiest place I could ever possibly access, tapping into that sacred joy I find only on trail. And I stay in that energy all morning long. The trail is clear, the mountains magnificent, the weather perfect. I could not ask for a more incredible experience.

Until I realize I am lost.

This realization comes suddenly, after what I'd assumed was the correct trail ends abruptly. I take out my phone to look at my GPS and realize that I'm pretty far from where I'm supposed to be. In fact, I might be a thousand feet *below* the correct trail. I have no idea where I went wrong. Perhaps the snowbanks I had to crawl around hid the relevant trail markers, and I simply got on the wrong path. Being so blissed out, I made the stupid mistake of not looking at my trail notes as frequently as I should have.

Checking the Gaia hiking app on my phone for the correct trail location, I begin to climb straight up, praying that the path will be clearly visible whenever I reach it. It's a straight vertical climb up the mountain, through tall grasses—painful for my legs and a bit scary. If something were to happen, I'm not sure anyone would find me on the remote mountainside. This motivates me to push harder, but as I continue to ascend, I realize my GPS is not working properly, and there's a chance this attempt at finding the trail might not end well.

When I reach the top of the mountain and still do not see where I'm supposed to go, panic sets in. Real panic. I'm not sure how to get myself either back to where I came from or to where I am heading. I'm completely alone on a mountain I'm not familiar with, with no trail in sight, no cell reception, and a malfunctioning GPS. I feel tears begin to well up in my eyes and fight to hold them at bay.

I get as high on the mountain slope as I can and pull out my route notes again. I should be able to see a glacial lake at this point. My guess is that it's going to be on the Kosovo side of the ridge, so as I make my way along the ridgeline, I keep looking down, desperately hoping to see water below. But no lake appears. Only mountains and valleys and towns, far in the distance.

My heart drops. I do not know what to do. This is a really, really bad situation.

But then, far off to the right and miles below where I stand, I spot the faintest hint of blue in the mountain valley. A lake. I quickly move farther up the ridge and notice faded remnants of trail blazes painted on the rocks. Whether or not this is *my* path, at least it is *a* path! I reach the top of the mountain to find a glorious view of the glacial lake below, but then once again, the path disappears.

I realize I need to head down the mountain, but I have five miles of downhill before I reach town, and I do not know the best route to get there. I desperately try to follow my GPS, but it keeps pointing me in odd directions. I try to focus on my breath because I know bad decisions are made when panic sets in. I just hope my GPS works well enough to lead me somewhere safe.

Eventually, I see a pole in the distance. A pole! I had seen poles the day before, marking the trail to the peak of Ljuboten. I jubilantly start walking toward the marker, not knowing if this truly indicates my path or merely highlights the border between Kosovo and North Macedonia, but I do not care. It marks a direction. A way to get the hell off this mountain and someplace where I can be found again. I begin the long journey down the mountainside until I once again see blazed rocks and seem to finally be back on the right trail.

I am going to be okay.

It takes a few hours for the panic to subside and the adrenaline to dissipate, but eventually, I'm able to sink back into enjoying the hike. When I'm finally at my hotel, showered and calmer, I remind myself that these situations are part of being a hiker. There will be times when the path is not clear and when it is vital for me to rely on my skills and experience. I need to always remember to trust that I can eventually find my way. All I'd needed was a reference point to help me arrive at a place of safety.

On one of my last days in North Macedonia, I am on a mountainside once again, but this time I'm strapped to a professional paraglider. Together, we run off the cliff and let the air current pull us high into the sky. My pilot masterfully guides us as we soar among the mountain crags and majestic peaks, with North Macedonia and all her grandeur laid out below. And though I once again find myself feeling slightly terrified as we make large sweeping circles through the sky, I challenge myself to let go, reminding myself that this experience is not about effort but surrender.

I take these final moments while airborne to reflect back on all the elements that have created the mosaic of this journey. The alarming leg pain I felt while still at home. The deep grief over whether or not I would heal. The ecstatic joy of my time on trail. And the deep terror when I could not find my way. Each of these experiences embodied a profound lesson in trust and tenacity and a reminder for me to search for the light, even when the darkness is unrelenting. As I take in my final view of the mountainous wonderland that has been both my home and my teacher, I feel such a sense of completion and gratitude and a new depth of resilience in my life. This was not an easy journey, but everything I went through was a powerful reminder of how supported I am in the world.

LOGISTICS

I booked my trip through the Natural Adventure Company (I chose their Via Dinarica in North Macedonia itinerary) and thought it was one of the best-planned trips I've ever taken. Ema, who runs the Macedonia Experiences, is truly the most wonderful person I have worked with while traveling. Her love for her country and her skill in ensuring that travelers have incredible experiences were unparalleled by anyone at any agency I've worked with before. She even took me to her tattooist for my dot tattoo! I honestly was sad to say goodbye to her at the end of my travels.

Choosing a Route

Though there are a variety of mountain ranges to explore throughout North Macedonia, I found the Shar Mountains extraordinarily beautiful. You can start your hike from the great mountain resort Popova Shapka and hike around and up to the peak of Titov Vruh. From there, I recommend hiring a transfer to take you to the Konak Hut from which you can hike around the Ljuboten area. I spent my last day hiking from the city of Skopje to the Millennium Cross and onwards to Mount Vodno, which was delightful (and a very easy trail to follow).

Getting to the Trailhead

North Macedonia's international airport is in the capital of Skopje. From there, you can arrange a car transfer into the Shar Mountains.

It's easy to book an in-country taxi to the beginning of any trail you wish to explore. Alternatively, if you hire the Natural Adventure Company, they will book all your transfers for you.

Length and Difficulty

The itinerary I completed was forty-one miles in five days. This was a seriously challenging hike that required some route finding, circumventing hundreds of feet of snow patches, and ascending thousands of feet in elevation. I would recommend this hike only for seasoned hikers.

Accommodations

For this hike, you'll stay in a combination of mountain huts and simple hotels. Camping is banned in the Shar Mountains.

Best Time to Hike

Snow is still abundant at the higher elevations in June, which necessitates some navigation, but I found it mostly manageable. However, I would recommend visiting anytime from July to October.

Pro Tips

All I can say is, *do this trip*. The beauty will astound you, and Macedonians are the kindest people. Also, I'd recommend taking a few days to visit Lake Ohrid at the end of your stay. The churches set against the lake backdrop are stunning, and the town is lively and serves delicious food.

If you do go to Lake Ohrid, definitely book a paragliding adventure. It is extraordinary to soar among the clouds after five days of hiking mountain peaks.

In 2019, Macedonia officially changed its name to the Republic of North Macedonia. Though this is the name you will see on official documents and maps, everyone I met in the country still preferred calling it Macedonia.

Finally, I strongly recommend wearing long pants for this hike because many areas of the trails were overgrown with stinging nettles. My legs were battle scarred at the end of my adventure, and I wished I had had better protection for my skin.

BOOKS

Travel Light in Macedonia: Hiking, Cozy Villages, and Crystal Clear Lakes by Ylva Johansson (independently published).

LOCAL LANGUAGE: MACEDONIAN

Thank you: Ви благодарам (vee blah-GOH-dah-rahm)
Please: ве молам (vee MOH-lahm)
I'm sorry: жал ми е (JHAL mi ay)

Macedonia was incredibly vegan-friendly, and there were many regional dishes that I adored. However, if I could pick one Macedonian dish to eat every day for the rest of my life, it would be *ajvar*. While there, I ate this dip three meals a day, and I still often eat it for a snack now that I'm back home.

AJVAR
(Serbian Roasted Red Pepper Dip)

Serves 6–8

INGREDIENTS

6 yellow, red, or orange bell peppers

1 small eggplant

3 tbsp extra virgin olive oil, divided

3 garlic cloves, roughly chopped

1 oz fresh chives

1 tbsp freshly squeezed lemon juice

1 tbsp red wine vinegar

¼ tsp crushed red pepper flakes

1 tsp sugar

salt and pepper to taste

DIRECTIONS

1. Heat oven to 450°F and arrange racks to the upper third. Halve each pepper, discarding stems and seeds. Place peppers cut side down on a baking sheet lined with foil.

2. Cut eggplant in half lengthwise and drizzle with about 1 tbsp of olive oil and a little salt. Place it cut side down on the baking sheet.

3. Roast peppers and eggplant until they are blackened and blistered and eggplant collapses when you press on it, about 30 minutes.

4. Remove eggplant and set aside to cool slightly. Remove peppers, place in a bowl, and cover with plastic wrap until peppers have slightly cooled, at least 5 minutes. Use a spoon or ice-cream scoop to remove eggplant pulp from the skin and discard skin.

5. Put eggplant in a food processor with 1 tbsp of olive oil and garlic. Pulse the eggplant a few times so it's roughly chopped.

6. Once peppers are cool enough to handle, peel them (reserving any juices that collect), discard the peel, and add peppers and 2–3 tbsp of pepper liquid to the food processor.

7. Pulse 5–8 times to chop coarsely. Stir in the lemon juice, vinegar, red pepper flakes, and sugar.

8. Taste, adding more sugar if it is a bit sour, and add salt and freshly ground black pepper if desired. Serve warm or at room temperature as a spread or condiment.

FREQUENTLY ASKED QUESTIONS

I anticipate that you probably have questions about both the feasibility and ethics of doing some of these hikes, so here's my attempt to address what might be on your mind.

1. How physically fit do you have to be?

It really depends on the trail you choose. Some of these hikes necessitate a moderate amount of fitness (such as the Caminos and the Dingle Way), and some require serious training time (like the Tour du Mont Blanc and Aniakchak Crater). I note the difficulty of each hike in the chapter headings. But remember: the beauty of hiking is that it's truly just about putting one foot in front of the other. Dedicating time at the gym (or, even better, on trail) is important, but you don't have to be super fit to be a strong hiker.

More essential than physical strength is mental fortitude. If you spend significant time on trail, you are most likely going to face challenges, such as exhaustion, getting lost, blisters, running out of water, and a variety of other mishaps along the way. Training your mind to be agile, resilient, and strong is as important as, if not more important than, a strong body.

2. How expensive is it to complete these treks?

International travel can be expensive, but I've found that once you arrive at your hiking destination, in-country costs can be minimal. Though airfare is consistently the biggest financial barrier to reaching remote hikes, here's a list of resources that can help you find cheaper options:

- Many sites offer inexpensive flight deals, such as Skyscanner, Kiwi, Kayak, Going (formerly Scott›s Cheap Flights), and Google Flights. Monitor these websites to find great deals.

- Be flexible with your travel dates and times. It tends to be less expensive to fly in the middle of the week or right after a major holiday. The time of day for your departure can also impact price. Be creative with your search criteria.

- Switch to an airline credit card. That way you can earn miles year-round from every purchase you make.

- Be flexible with your destination airport. Many budget airlines fly to airports located a bit outside of major cities. See if you can find a great deal to a nearby location and then take a bus or train to your final destination.

- Consider booking with a discount airline when one is available, such as Southwest, JetBlue, Ryanair, and easyJet.

Though the cost of international travel can be daunting, by following airfare websites, having flexible travel dates and times, and once in-country, being creative about food and accommodations, you can travel for much less than you'd expect.

3. But money is not the only issue; isn't air travel bad for the environment?

I wish I could offer a list of all the ways you can make air travel less injurious to the planet, but unfortunately, the reality is that anytime we fly, we are harming the environment. There's just no way around that. Carbon offsets, though not a solution, can at least help. For those unfamiliar with carbon offsets, companies calculate the environmental impact of your flight and create a corresponding dollar amount they will invest in sustainable environmental projects, such as planting trees. Search online to find a company whose mission matches your values and download their app to use each time you fly.

4. What about the role of privilege?

The question of privilege is something I think about all the time when I travel. I understand that where I come from and the color of my skin afford me privileges abroad that many others, including those close to me in my life and in my community, do not have. Some friends have shared their opinion that it's simply irresponsible to travel to certain places at all—they believe that if a country is facing economic hardship, visiting that country as a tourist is an exploitative act. I have listened to their arguments and honor the roots and reasoning behind them, and I do recognize that there's some truth to this idea. But I also know that tourism plays a significant role in elevating the economies of the places I travel, so by not traveling there, funds are not reaching people who need them. In the end, you have to decide if international travel aligns with your values.

If you do decide to travel, I believe there are ways to be an intentional traveler whose presence can have at least a somewhat positive impact. Some of my favorite practices while traveling include staying at locally owned hotels, arranging travel through local operators, and to the extent possible, making sure that people employed by the trekking agency are paid a living wage. It's also a good practice to learn about local customs and norms and to honor those while there.

Indeed, I recommend prioritizing the local economy wherever you go. Instead of shopping in big chain stores, try to find farmers markets or small, local grocery stores (which tend to have more delicious produce anyway!). Avoid franchise and foreign-owned restaurants. And be sure to tip generously.

You can take your positive impact a step further by volunteering or finding local nonprofits to support. Be kind to everyone you meet. Be generous with your smiles and compliments. Ask questions instead of making assumptions. And—so important—leave the trail cleaner than you found it.

Of course, there's also the privilege of being able-bodied. Having faced several injuries in my life, I recognize the challenge of modifying outdoor experiences to make them accessible (though this certainly pales in comparison to the obstacles faced by those with significant mobility challenges). I realize that I'm extremely fortunate to have a body that currently has the ability to hike. But with age, I've become more and more aware that each of us is on borrowed time. The more we take care of our bodies (stretching, hydrating, taking breaks from hard exertion), the more years we should have to spend outside.

For people who face physical or emotional barriers that might impact their ability to be on trail, there are great organizations, like Disabled Hikers, that create group hikes and offer resources for differently abled individuals. Check out Disabled Hikers online or search for similar groups in your community. Another site worth exploring is Planet Abled, a woman-owned tour company that provides accessible group tours and customized trips in more than forty destinations across Europe and Asia.

5. How daunting is the language barrier?

Another undeniable privilege is the fact that English is a global language. Yet it's true that the farther you travel from larger cities or well-known tourist destinations, the less English is spoken. In these situations, I've happily harnessed the power of Google Translate. This app translates typed or spoken sentences (keep them short to facilitate translation) into written or spoken speech. It can even translate menus and signs with the camera tool. I highly recommend getting familiar with the app before you go. I've found it to be invaluable.

Before I leave on a trip, I also memorize a few words in the language of the country I'm about to visit. I find "please," "thank you," and "I'm sorry" go a long way in helping create rapport. For that reason, I include these phrases at the end of each chapter.

6. Isn't it lonely to hike solo? Is it safe?

If you're open to the challenge of traveling alone but find the idea intimidating, there are a few strategies that can help. First, be kind to yourself. If you're unaccustomed to spending a lot of time alone, it can be daunting and downright lonely. But instead of abandoning your solo travels at the first sign of struggle, congratulate yourself for trying something new. Then let yourself feel whatever emotions arise. Being present with what is in your heart is a self-honoring, healing act. And the more you allow challenging feelings to simply emerge, the more quickly they'll pass and create room for joy to take their place.

It's also important to make sure to talk to at least one person each day whenever possible. Even a brief conversation can bring buoyancy to a lonely heart. Ask to join other hikers at meals. Also, download some entertaining podcasts or books for the times you need a distraction from your own thoughts. If you get really lonely or bored, think of the people you love and mentally send each of them gratitude. And remember, the more time you spend in the quiet, the more you will hear the wisdom of your own heart.

Some might push back and say that it's too unsafe or simply unwise to hike alone, and that argument has merit. It is better to be on trail with others in case something goes wrong. More people present means you're less likely to get lost, mugged, or assaulted or to have an unpleasant animal encounter. And if you become injured or ill, it can be lifesaving to have others there to help.

But there are also many glorious reasons to travel and hike solo, as long as you make sure someone knows where you are (always leave a detailed itinerary with someone back home). I find that being alone while traveling offers exquisite freedom. Every day is a practice in acknowledging your own personal needs and following your own truths. And by being silent on trail, you're able to hear the quiet messages the mountains may have to share.

Moreover, when you do want connection, solo travelers have the advantage of being able to forge deep friendships with other hikers more easily, as their attention is not directed to a friend or partner with whom they are traveling. And facing challenges while you're on your own forces you to grow as a person and a hiker. You'll find reserves of strength you never knew you had and come out on the other side more resilient than before.

For me, going solo means coming home to a more expanded version of myself.

Of course, it's important to do in-depth research about the potential safety concerns of your hiking destination. There are certain places in the world I wouldn't feel comfortable hiking solo, whereas others might. Do some deep soul-searching when contemplating a trip to decide if being there by yourself would be a fit for you. And if you want to try solo hiking but don't want to be completely alone, you could start by choosing a more popular hike, such as the Camino Frances, Everest Base Camp, or the Torres del Paine, where there'll always be others around you.

For those for whom solo hiking isn't appealing and who would like to trek with others, I recommend booking as a part of a group through Distant Journeys, the Natural Adventure Company, and KE Travel.

7. And now the big question: Why did I choose these specific hikes?

There is no grand, overarching theme for how I plan my hikes, and there doesn't have to be for you either. Often, when I hear someone mention a hike, I look it up and sometimes just know that I need to explore that trail. Or I'll read an article in a travel blog or magazine and feel this bubbling excitement at the idea of being in that particular place. Outside of the "Alphabet Travel" project with my friend Hilary, there's nothing systematic about where I choose to go—just a feeling that I should be there. Also, asking other hikers about their favorite treks has opened up a whole world of bucket-list destinations for me!

My dot tattoos continue to grow as a tribute to:
each trail I have walked,
each wisdom I have gained,
and each lesson I have learned
while walking.

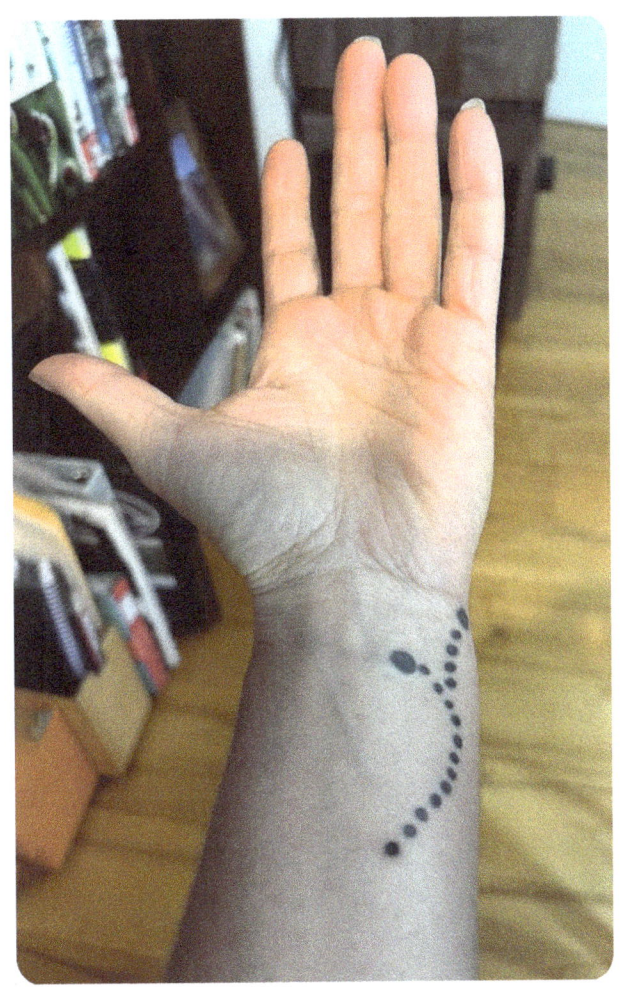

Additional Hikes

The hikes detailed in this book are the ones that have offered me the greatest life lessons. But many other trails have gifted me their beauty, their challenges, their awe, and their wonder. Here are some of the other places I've had the privilege of walking and whose trails have etched lasting maps upon my heart.

▲ Mount Rogers Hike, Grayson Highlands, Virginia, USA
Ahu Akivi, Easter Island, Chile ▶

Four Loop Pass, Colorado, USA ▶

Cramer Lakes, Sawtooth Mountains, Idaho, USA ▲
◀ Plitvice Lakes National Park, Croatia

Wheeler Peak, New Mexico, USA ▲
◀ Ilulissat Icefjord Loop, Greenland

▲ Virginia Triple Crown Hike, Virginia, USA

Mt. Kollata, Montenegro ▶

▲ Aesbech River Trail, Luxembourg
Gjov Cliffs Hike, Faroe Islands ▶

▲ Tiger's Nest Monastery Hike, Bhutan

◄ Fjadrargljufur Canyon, Iceland

Kasteelspoort, Table Mountain, South Africa ▲

▲ Kilimanjaro, Tanzania, Africa

Velka Svistovka Peak, High Tatras, Slovakia ▶

Rae Lakes Loop, King's Canyon, USA ▲

▲ Hike to Wat Phra That Doi Suthep, Chiang Mai, Thailand

▲ Alta Via 1, Dolomites, Italy

Xela to Lake Atitlan, Guatemala ▶

Helen Lake Trail, BANFF, Canada ▲

▲ Poon Hill Trek, Annapurna Mountain Range, Nepal

Accursed Mountains, Albania ▶

◄ Golden Canyon, Death Valley, California, USA

Additional Hikes / 169

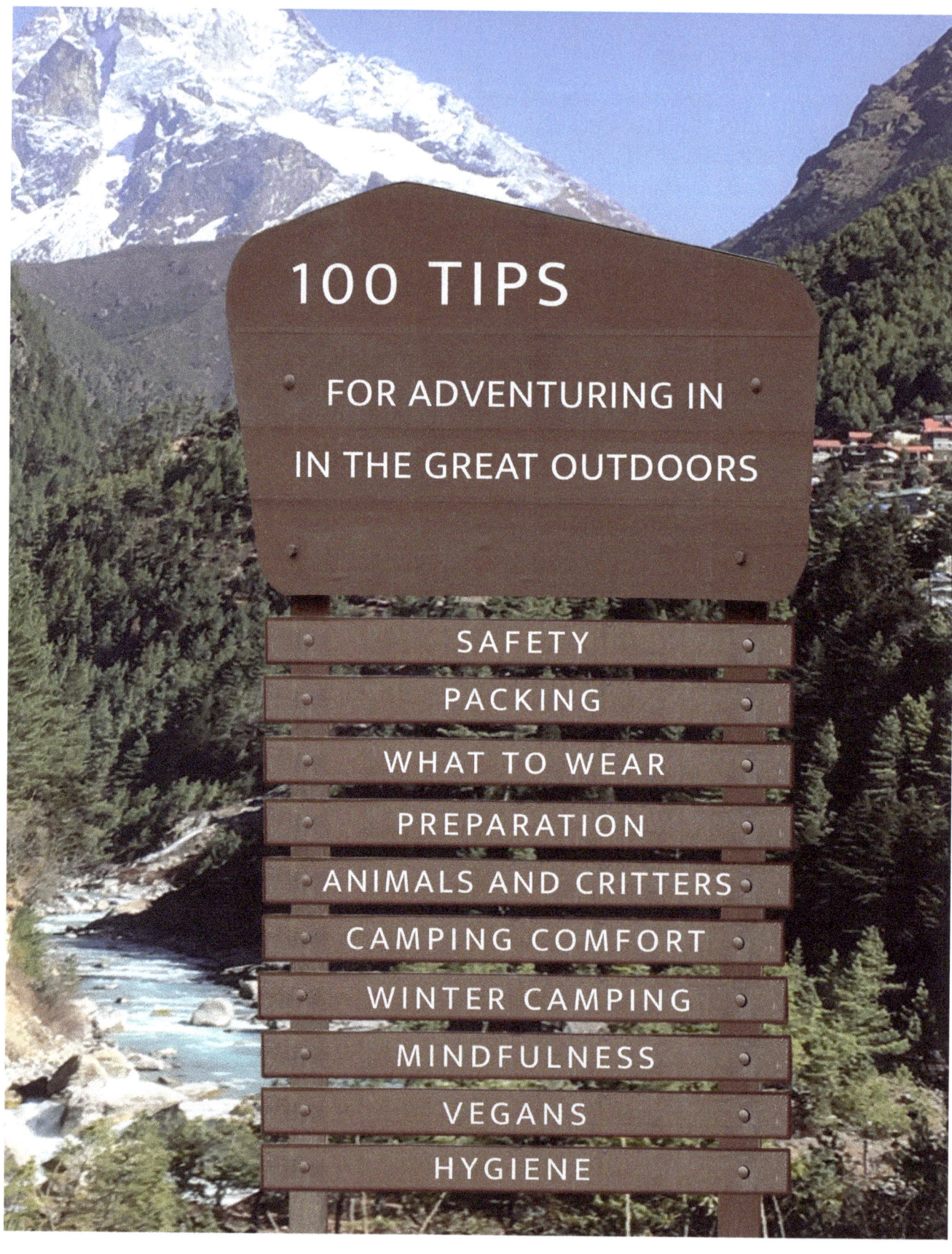

Recently, I decided to hike to John Rock in Pisgah National Forest. As I climbed the gentle ascent to the rock face with a stunning 180-degree view of the surrounding Blue Ridge Mountains, I reflected on the first time I made this hike. It was eight years ago, and I'd just moved to Asheville, North Carolina, from the concrete jungle of Chicago. And though I'd hiked Kilimanjaro just a few years earlier, I still had no idea how to spend a night outside by myself.

Determined to celebrate the Jewish New Year witnessing the sun setting over the mountains of my new hometown, I began assembling my camping essentials. Of course, my pack was too heavy. My clothes were all wrong. And the campsite had no water, so I had to carry my own from the parking lot up the three miles to the mountain's ridge.

Even though I was far from comfortable, something in me transformed that night. Once the crowds of day hikers left and I was alone to savor the mountain air, the colorful sunset, and the gentle sounds of frogs and birds, I found peace—a profound, integrated, internal harmony that directly connected me to the magic of the outdoors.

Today, hiking and backpacking are a larger part of my identity than I could have ever imagined. I spend hours poring over hiking books and potential trails and plan most of my vacations around which mountains I want to climb. I wake up early on the weekends to claim the quiet of mountain paths as my own. And along the way, I've learned one or two (or one hundred) things that make me much more comfortable (and safe!) in the wild.

This list compiles a few of those lessons. Some I have discovered on my own, often through much trial and error. Many I have blatantly stolen from my fellow hikers. And others remain a work in progress. Still, most of these lessons were hard earned, and I'm excited to share them with you to support you on your upcoming adventures.

As you continue (or begin) your outdoor journeying, may the trails you walk be filled with beauty. May you know yourself as someone who is strong and capable. May you show humility in the face of the power of nature. And may you learn more about the magnificent person you are each time your feet touch the trail.

10
TIPS
FOR SAFETY

1 **Designate an accountability person.** Anytime you hike, always let someone know where you're going and when you expect to be home. It's also helpful to share a "definitely call the police if you don't hear from me by this specific time" deadline. Even for short hikes, it's important that someone confirms you make it back safely.

2 **Back it up.** In case your phone dies, have a battery backup. This is especially crucial if you're using AllTrails or a similar app as your main navigation tool. Anker makes a fantastic lightweight battery that holds a 10,000mAh charge.

3 **Track fast-moving weather.** Be sure to check the weather forecast before you go and, if possible, continually while on trail. Even if a day starts off with sunshine and blue skies, a potential storm might be making its way to where you're hiking. Research if there's the possibility of flash floods, and never be on a ridgeline when there's lightning. If you do hear thunder or see lightning, get off the ridge as fast as you can, and try to find shelter. If shelter is not available, seek protection in a valley or on terrain away from isolated trees or tall objects. And make sure metal hiking poles are at least one hundred feet away from you!

4 **Map it.** It's always a good idea to have a downloaded map of your hiking area on your phone. I never go into the woods without downloading my destination on the AllTrails app. When you purchase AllTrails's Pro option for $30 a year, you can use your trail map even when offline. The cost might seem substantial for an app, but not spending hours lost in the woods? Priceless.

5 **Hydrate regularly.** Dehydration can be deadly on trail. Always carry a water filter, identify water sources before you go, and if your map shows significant mileage between creeks or streams, make sure to carry additional water.

6 **Go analog.** Sometimes phones fail, which is why a compass and paper map are indispensable as backup navigation tools. But these resources are useless if you don't know how to use them properly. I strongly recommend taking a navigation course at REI and making sure to frequently practice what you learn.

7 **Don't be a hangry hiker.** When hiking, you will burn more calories than you might anticipate. Having a low caloric reserve is detrimental for both your body and mind. Always carry an extra bar or two in case you need a boost.

8 **Be ready for "just in case."** Carrying a first-aid kit is essential. However, it might be beside the point if you don't know how to use the contents. Take some time to familiarize yourself with how to use each item *before* you get on trail. Additionally, I recommend taking a basic class in wilderness first aid to learn how to address any minor medical emergencies that might arise.

9 **Have happy feet.** Your feet are one of your greatest assets on trail, and the more you take care of them, the happier you'll be. The second you feel a hot spot or blister emerging, stop and take care of it. Remove your shoes and socks, apply moleskin (or my favorite miracle blister preventer, Compeed), and you'll be ready to get on your way!

10 **Stay on trail.** Another good rule of thumb is to always stay on the designated trail, especially if you're new to hiking. Not only is it easy to get lost if you leave the path, but you're also more likely to unwittingly step on a snake or stinging insect while bushwhacking away from the cleared path.

10 TIPS

FOR PROPER PACKING

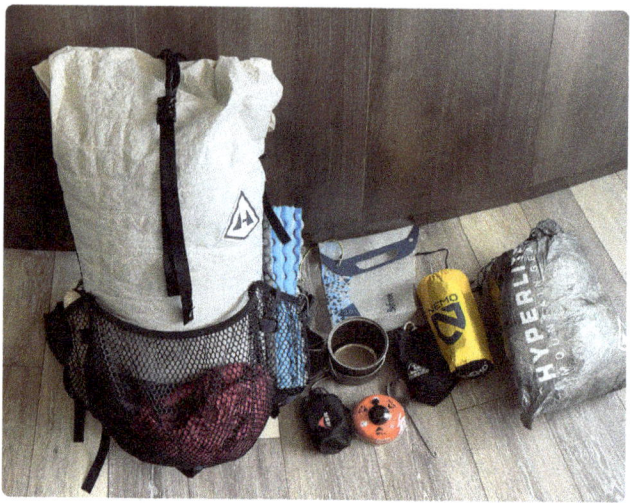

1. **Go light.** Regarding your pack, I cannot say this enough—*go light*! The harder the hike, the more you'll lament every extra ounce on your back. Buy the lightest version of your essentials, and opt for miniatures whenever possible (this works well for toothpaste, bug spray, hand sanitizer, etc.).

2. **Strategize.** Put items that you won't need until camp (sleeping bag, tent) at the very bottom of your bag and the things you'll use throughout the day (food, clothing layers) at the top.

3. **Unleash your inner MacGyver.** Carry a multi-tool with scissors and a knife. Don't bring a huge Leatherman as the weight is unnecessary. I personally use the Leatherman Micra, which weighs less than two ounces.

4. **Balance on your back.** Make sure your pack feels as comfortable as possible on your back. Placing heavier items toward the part of your pack that touches your back will help you stay balanced while hiking.

5. **Stash it.** Make the most out of hip-belt storage. I like to keep my phone in one pocket and other items I'll use throughout the day, such as lip balm, sunblock, a snack, and perhaps some anti-chafing cream, in the other.

6. **Defend your down.*** Don't let your down items get wet. The main drawback of down is that once it is wet, it will not keep you warm. I keep my sleeping bag and down clothes in waterproof bags and put them inside my waterproof pack for multiple layers of protection.

7 **Get organized.** I find it's easy to locate things quickly in my pack when they're organized into different-colored, lightweight bags. Use small bags to separate food, electronics, clothes, and toiletries.

8 **Stay upright.** Anytime I have ten pounds or more on my back, I use hiking poles to improve my stability. Not only have poles kept me upright hundreds of times when I would've otherwise face-planted, they also help reduce the physical impact of weight on the body by up to 25 percent. My favorite is Leki's Cressida Antishock Poles.

9 **Keep it dry.** Make sure to have a waterproof bag for the outside of any pack that isn't itself waterproof, and ensure that it's easily accessible in case of a sudden downpour. If the forecast calls for severe storms, it's also not a bad idea to line the inside of your pack with something as simple as a thick garbage bag. Keep your rain gear in the outside pocket of your pack, along with an additional layer for warmth. That way, if you get caught in a rainstorm (or just get cold), you don't have to dig far in your pack to find what you need.

10 **Purify.** It's critical to carry a great water filter and keep it easily accessible. I personally love the BeFree Filter by Katadyn—it has excellent water flow and weighs almost nothing. Use a small bungee cord to hang the filter from a tree branch to facilitate filtration and flow. And don't forget: the night before leaving on a trip, soak the filter in water, so it doesn't dry out.

---

* *Not all vegans feel comfortable using down products, but if you do, there are two ways to make it more ethically palatable: you can buy used or recycled down items or, if buying new, do so from places that ethically source their down, such as Western Mountaineering.*

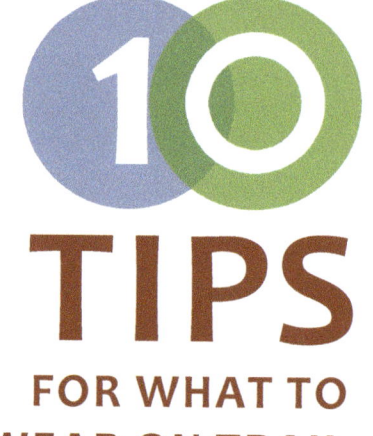

10 TIPS

FOR WHAT TO WEAR ON TRAIL

1 **Bigger isn't better.** There's a ton of buzz about the best shoes to wear hiking, but something everyone agrees on is the heavier your shoe, the more your feet will suffer. A seriously hefty hiking boot is necessary only if you have a ton of weight on your back, or you're doing some intense off-trail trekking. If neither of these applies to you, consider a trail runner. I adore Altra shoes (which I've worn on trails throughout the world) because they have a wider toe box for comfort. Their Lone Peak Hiker is the best of both worlds—a trail runner base with added ankle support.

2 **Accessorize your shoes.** There are two foot-oriented issues that truly irritate me on trail—the first is rocks getting in my shoes, and the second is shoelaces coming untied. Fortunately, Dirty Girl Gaiters solve both. Available in a fabulous array of colors and designs, these lightweight gaiters fit around your ankle and attach to your shoe, keeping your socks free of debris and your laces secure.

3 **Wear performance pants.** I highly recommend wearing actual hiking pants. Though workout leggings may be cuter, they don't breathe as well and take much longer to dry (and they have no pockets to hold your essentials!). And because it also doesn't dry quickly, you want to avoid cotton (especially jeans).

4 **Upgrade the undies.** I recommend investing in a few pairs of good hiking underwear, like those made by ExOfficio. Their underwear is lightweight, breathable, quick drying, and most important, odor resistant. One pair can last several days between washings.

5 **Be sweat-free.** If you are like me, you sweat. A lot. Keeping sweat out of your eyes is important for both comfort and safety (so you can see where you're going, obviously, but also spy any rogue rocks or roots waiting to literally trip you up!). This is why I always wear a Buff or other synthetic headband to keep my face as dry as possible.

6 **Let's talk about socks (baby).** Socks are crucial in your quest for happy feet. I am a double-protection person and wear a sock liner plus a light performance sock. This combination has kept my feet blister-free for years. For liners, I recommend Injinji Toesocks as they have separate toe sections, which helps prevent rubbing. Put a Darn Tough Coolmax Hiker sock over them, and you are good to go.

7 **Cover up.** The sun can be a sneaky foe, burning exposed skin even on the cloudiest days. Make sure to always apply sunscreen, and ideally, wear a good hat to cover your face. I like a visor since it protects my face and allows me to wear my hair in my signature pigtails. If you would like to take sun protection to the next level, wear a floppy hat to cover the back of your neck as well.

8 **Support the "ladies."** Hikers with larger breasts should have a good hiking bra to keep the ladies secured. I recommend Patagonia's Barely Bra, which fits well, is fast drying, and is easy to get off at the end of a long day.

9 **Track it.** I wear a smart watch because I like to keep track of my mileage and pace. When I know just how far I have left to go and how fast I am walking, I can pace myself accordingly and create fun goals like "five miles until the next chocolate break!"

10 **Love your layers.** When I'm on trail, my body temperature changes constantly—typically from cold at the beginning, to warm while working my way up a mountain, and back to cold as soon as I take a break. This is why layers are my best friend. I like to have a T-shirt (regardless of the temperature outside), a long-sleeved synthetic shirt, a fleece, and a puffer jacket either on my body or easily accessible in my pack.

10 THINGS

TO DO BEFORE EVERY HIKE

1   **Research the rules.** Before you hit any trail, check to see if a permit is required. Nothing is more disappointing than driving a good distance to your dream hike only to find that it requires preregistration.

2   **Know before you go.** Sometimes trails are closed for various reasons— avalanches, trail maintenance, downed trees, controlled burns, and overuse, for example. Read up on your target trail before you set out to make sure it's open for use. You can check park websites for up-to-date trail information.

3   **Get informed.** Before every trip, I voraciously read the AllTrails comments about the trail I'm about to hike. Knowing what others have experienced helps me prepare for potential obstacles and ensures that I am aware of cool hidden features (crashed planes, waterfalls, moonshining vehicles) to be found along the way.

4   **Work those legs.** The more physically fit you are, the more enjoyable your hike will be. Though the best way to train for a hike is to actually hike, any exercise that increases leg strength (squats, lunges, box jumps, rowing) is well worth your time.

5   **Download your maps.** Make sure you have downloaded the map(s) you will need *before* you get to your hike (where there may not be cell service). Hiking applications such as AllTrails and Gaia allow you to download maps beforehand and show you where you are on a map relative to where you should be.

6 **Drink up.** It's critical to identify the water sources along your route. By figuring out mileage between creeks and streams, you can assess how much water you'll need to carry. Never assume that you'll easily find water if you're high up on a ridgeline. And even if water looks pristine, always purify it.

7 **Tell a friend.** *Always* let someone know where you're going and what time to expect to hear from you at your hike's completion. And I mean always. Even if you're only hiking a few miles, you never know what might happen in the woods.

8 **List it.** It's nice to have prepared packing lists, especially if you are a newbie hiker. I recommend creating a list for what to bring on a day hike and a list for what to bring on an overnight hike. Make sure you always have a first-aid kit, a fire source, snacks, layers, and a battery pack.

9 **Treat yourself.** Even before leaving your house, decide what your post-hike celebratory meal will be. Not only will this eliminate having to figure out what to eat when you're exhausted and smelly and hangry, but it will also give you something to daydream about on trail. When I was hiking the Smokies, sometimes the only thing that kept me climbing those mountain peaks was visualizing the vegan pizza I would devour when I got back home.

10 **Be fuel savvy.** This one seems obvious, but make sure you have a full tank of gas before you leave for the woods. Finding a reliable gas station in rural areas can be difficult.

10 WAYS

TO PREPARE FOR ANIMALS AND CRITTERS

1 **Get the 411.** The fear of animals and insects should never be a reason to stay home! Just be aware and prepared. I recommend getting informed well before you're on trail, so you'll know how to handle different animals you might encounter. My favorite book on this subject is *Look Big: And Other Tips for Surviving Animal Encounters of All Kinds* by Rachel Levin. It is gorgeously illustrated and a joy to read.

2 **Grin and bear it.** Bears are quite possibly the most intimidating animal for people to encounter, despite the fact that they are usually far more afraid of us than we are of them. The number-one step to ensure a bear-free experience is to hang your food and toiletries up high when you get to camp. Find a tree with a branch about nine feet off the ground and throw a bear bag over the branch a few feet from the trunk. I like Liberty Mountain's Easy-to-Throw Bear Bag Hanging Kit because it includes a bag you can fill with rocks to help get the rope over the branch. When you hang the bag, make sure there's at least a foot between your bag and the branch to prevent rodents from getting to your goodies. A great rule of thumb is that if something has a scent, however faint, it gets hung up high.

3 **Keep 'em aware.** Another way to stay safe from bears is to never take them by surprise. Every single time I go around a blind curve, I sing a song to make my presence known (my favorite is my personalized version of "Hey bear... you're an all-star...get your game on..."). Wearing a bear bell is less effective because you want the bear to know that you are a human, not a bird. If you're hiking in an area with a lot of bears, carry a can of bear spray. Just make sure it's easily accessible and to read the directions before use (so you don't spray someone in the face as my dad did to me once).

4 **Watch the clock.** Try to avoid hiking at dawn or dusk when animals are most active.

5 **Foil flying foes.** As far as insects go, yellowjacket stings are the worst! I have stepped on nests two times, and the pain was excruciating. Though sometimes a nest is impossible to spot, you should be alert for them in hollow trees, hanging from branches, in or under fallen logs, or in the ground. Know that yellowjackets tend to be attracted to bright colors, sweet smells, and swift movements, so plan and act accordingly.

6 **Don't pick up hitchhikers.** An unfortunate reality of outdoor adventuring is the presence of ticks. To reduce your risk, spray Permethrin on your clothing. Wearing long pants and a hat is also helpful, so you don't have to pick ticks off your ankles or out of your hair (believe me—not a fun experience).

7 **Scan for parasites.** At the end of every day, do a tick check all over your body, especially in dark nooks and crannies like behind your ears and in your armpits. Carry a Tick Key in case a tick becomes embedded in your skin; this tool allows you to remove the entire tick, embedded head and all, which is vital to avoid any tick-borne illnesses and challenging to do with just your hands.

8 **Stay away from slithering friends.** It's a good rule of thumb to never poke your head in an empty tree trunk! This one might seem obvious, but I once put my head inside a hollow tree to investigate an interesting noise coming from within and came face-to-face with a rattlesnake. Not my brightest moment. Stay away from hollowed trees, and when you step over a fallen tree, make sure a snake isn't lounging on the other side.

9 **Step mindfully.** To avoid snakes, be aware of your foot placement. Snakes are highly skilled at blending in, especially in piles of leaves and under and around downed logs. When walking over a log, put your hiking stick down first, so a snake will strike that instead of your leg.

10 **Lose the moose.** And if you're hiking in moose country, be careful—they can be quite aggressive. In fact, most animal attacks in the wild involve moose, not bears or mountain lions. If you do see a moose, give it plenty of space, and if appropriate, calmly walk away.

10 TIPS

FOR BEING MORE COMFORTABLE AT CAMP

1 **Find your foot bliss.** After a long day on trail, nothing feels better than taking off smelly socks and wet shoes and putting something clean on your feet. Though some think the extra weight is unnecessary, I find that a pair of lightweight waterproof shoes are worth every ounce (you can also use them for stream crossings). I personally swear by Vivobarefoot Women's Ultra III Synthetic Trainers.

2 **Protect what is sacred.** On my trip to Alaska, I was introduced to the concept of "sacred socks." These are simply socks (preferably the fuzzy kind) that *never* leave the inside of your tent. Never! By keeping this special pair of socks protected, they will always stay dry and cozy. Your feet will thank you each night when they slip into something super comfy and warm.

3 **Throw a pillow party.** In the hiking community, people debate the necessity of bringing a pillow. Some think you should save a few ounces and make do with a stuff sack full of your clothes. However, I find a pillow invaluable, as it significantly increases your odds of a decent night's sleep. I recommend one with deep grooves to keep your head in place, such as Sea to Summit's Aeros Ultralight Inflatable Pillow.

4 **Wind it down.** It's nice to have some type of entertainment to help you wind down before bedtime. I always make sure to download books from Amazon or Libro onto the Kindle app on my phone, so I can curl up and enjoy a good read in my tent. Some prefer carrying AirPods to use with the Audible app or to watch shows they've downloaded on their phones.

5 **Pamper yourself.** Bring one or two small luxury items that will make you feel a bit pampered at the end of a long day. My suggestions include peppermint foot salve, bathing wipes, a small bottle of essential oil, or Herban Essential's Lavender Towelettes.

6 **Find the light.** Since you'll want to bring both a beanie and a headlamp, why not combine them? A beanie with a built-in rechargeable LED light is a great way to stay warm and have easy, hands-free illumination at the same time.

7 **Soap it up.** I highly recommend bringing a travel-size bottle of Dr. Bronner's Pure-Castile Liquid Soap to wash everything from your hands to your dishware (the Dr. Bronner website boasts eighteen suggested uses).

8 **Salt is life.** Drinking electrolytes with salt is a great treat at the end of the day and helps your muscles recover. I am in love with the flavors by LMNT.

9 **Pack your PJs.** I commend people who lighten their pack by wearing their hiking clothes as their sleeping clothes, but the one time I tried it, I hated every minute of it! For me, sleeping in a pair of lightweight pajama bottoms (Gap has great options) and a clean shirt makes all the difference and is worth every ounce.

10 **Git 'er done.** As soon as you arrive at camp, I strongly recommend setting everything up, even if you are tired—pitch your tent, hang your bear bag, and set up your kitchen. Once all that is taken care of, you can spend the rest of your evening relaxing, worry-free.

COLD-WEATHER HACKS FOR WINTER CAMPING

1 **Snuggle up.** Spending a night shivering in the woods is the best way to ensure you'll never want to backpack in the cold again. If you plan on spending a few nights outside in weather below 40 degrees Fahrenheit (about 4 degrees Celsius), I highly recommend investing in a 15-degree or 0-degree sleeping bag. I personally love my REI Magma 15.

2 **Get warm, stay warm.** Down filling* will keep you warmer when your body temperature is already warm, since down traps pockets of warm air close to the skin. Therefore, try to heat up your body before you get into a down sleeping bag. Doing a few jumping jacks or push-ups before cuddling up means your bag will get you warmer faster.

3 **Line it up.** If you're like me and sleep cold, a sleeping-bag liner can add a little boost of delightful warmth (up to 10 degrees!). I personally love Appalachian Gear Company's All-Paca Sleeping Bag Liner.

4 **Keep your electronics toasty.** One thing I've learned the hard way is that electronics don't like cold weather either. When temperatures dip, keep your battery pack, phone, and smart watch in your sleeping bag with you to prolong battery life. It also helps to put your water filter in the sleeping bag to prevent it from freezing.

5 **Sleep smart.** Many people wear long underwear as their camp clothes in winter, but I'm a huge fan of lightweight fleece pajama bottoms. It feels almost festive to put them on at day's end. I also bring a pair of down booties to keep my feet toasty.

6 **Warm your extremities.** It's definitely worth it to bring a few packs of hand and feet warmers. They're lightweight and a great source of extra heat on particularly cold days.

7 **Fan the flames.** Cold evenings are more enjoyable around a fire. To facilitate fire building, bring along a couple of cotton balls that have been dipped in Vaseline. They're delightfully flammable and weigh almost nothing.

8 **Sleep with a hot friend.** For extra help warming up as you fall asleep, before you go to bed, fill your water bottle with hot water and place it in your sleeping bag.

9 **Go one last time.** Be sure to pee before you go to bed! I have no idea if there's scientific backing for this, but I always feel warmer if my bladder is empty. Also, peeing before you get in your bag means you're less likely to have to brave the cold to go in the middle of the night.

10 **Keep it R-rated.** Your sleeping pad is essential in keeping your body warm. A sleeping pad's R-value measures its ability to resist heat transfer and is rated on a scale from 0 to 7 for portable models. The higher the pad's R-value, the warmer you'll be. Make sure the value is at least above a 4 for cold-weather camping. I really like Therm-a-Rest's NeoAir Xtherm for winter.

---

* *Not all vegans feel comfortable using down products, but if you do, there are two ways to make it more ethically palatable: you can buy used or recycled down items or, if buying new, do so from places that ethically source their down, such as Western Mountaineering.*

MINDFUL PRACTICES TO ELEVATE YOUR TRAIL EXPERIENCE

1 **Set an intention.** There's something about mindfulness and hiking. The more thoughtfulness you put into your hike, the more you will get out of your time on trail. I like to set an intention before I start a trek, so I have something to ponder, let go of, or invite in while I'm walking.

2 **Look up.** Sometimes I get really bogged down in my thoughts and forget that there's a big, beautiful world that is so much greater than whatever I'm going through. When I remember to look up—into the treetops, at a mountain summit, or up at the clouds—as simple as it sounds, it brings me out of my head and into the world.

3 **Be a steward.** Part of feeling connected to the magic of the outdoors is to honor it by leaving the trail better than you found it. I try to pick up a few pieces of trash each time I hike to be a better steward of the beauty around me.

4 **Find your quiet.** If you're comfortable with or prefer being alone on trail, try to find less popular hikes. The AllTrails app highlights how crowded a trail may be, which helps plan for alone time.

5 **Wake up early.** For me, hikes are most enjoyable when it is quiet. Therefore, I find it is worth getting up a bit earlier to get on trail before others to savor that delicious outdoor solitude.

6 **Respect others.** Being aware of trail etiquette creates good vibes with other hikers. Remember that people hiking uphill have the right of way. It's also a good idea to keep your voice down and to always listen to music with headphones rather than an external speaker.

7 **Pace it.** Once while hiking with a group of extremely fit people, I was struggling to keep up on a particularly steep hill. The person leading the trek pulled me aside and kindly reminded me to "hike my own hike," for which I was grateful. By letting go of expectations on trail, you can really sink into your own best experience, which includes honoring the needs of your body.

8 **Wrap your mind around it.** I love any good book that helps me increase my awareness of, and gratitude for, my time on trail. Recently, I truly enjoyed reading *Trail Mix: Wit & Wisdom from the Outdoors* by Corinne Gaffner Garcia, a beautiful collection of quotes about hiking and the outdoors.

9 **Reflect.** At the end of each hike, I take a quiet moment to thank the trail. I reflect on what made that hike special (solitude, things I saw, thoughts I had, people I met) and set an intention to carry the lessons from that hike in my heart.

10 **Notice your surroundings.** Nature is the best tool for honing your mindfulness practice. Remember to take the time to notice the feel of the wind on your face, be aware of your heartbeat, and walk with the rhythm of your breath.

10
TIPS
FOR VEGANS
ON TRAIL

1 **Eat smart.** It doesn't have to be a challenge to eat vegan while on trail. The company Outdoor Herbivore has, hands down, the most delicious prepackaged vegan food I have come across. Their dinners are hearty, filling, and the perfect size for one person. And their lunches require only cold water to prepare, so they're great for a quick and easy meal.

2 **Bring snacks.** Make sure to have a variety of simple snacks on hand, so you can keep your caloric intake up during your trek. Personally, I enjoy having one sweet and one savory treat to enjoy while I'm hiking. My go-to sweet treat is a bar by Kate's Real Food (you can actually pronounce all the ingredients!). My savory choice is Bada Bean Bada Boom dehydrated, flavored fava beans.

3 **Pack some protein.** Wild Garden offers small packets of hummus that do not require refrigeration. Throw a few in your pack for a helping of heart-healthy protein.

4 **Cherish your chickpeas.** If you are on a hut-to-hut hike and find yourself walking through a town in need of protein, grab a can of chickpeas. They are super hearty and can be eaten straight from the can or sprinkled on salads or pasta for a protein boost.

5 **Spice it up.** Food can sometimes taste bland when it hasn't been prepared in your own fabulous kitchen. To fix this, get spicy! Most hot sauces are available in small packets (like ketchup and mustard). Carry a few of these, so you can easily add heat to any meal.

6 **Have a cuppa comfort.** Nothing says "delight" at the end of a cold day on trail like a vegan hot chocolate. Fortunately, even companies like Swiss Miss now offer a vegan version. Throw a few packets in your bag for an after-dinner treat.

7 **Share your ethics.** If traveling internationally, I recommend learning how to say "I am vegan" in the local language. If that doesn't translate, people usually understand "I am vegetarian," and then you can expand upon that with "no eggs, milk, cheese, or butter." Use the Google Translate app to find the right words.

8 **Chocolate is always a good idea.** Always pack your favorite vegan chocolate (which is hopefully not too prone to melting). I personally love Hu chocolate bars, which are vegan and paleo and come in mouthwatering flavors, like Cashew Butter + Raspberry and Vanilla Crunch.

9 **Go nuts!** Nuts are a hiking vegan's best friend. They go well on almost any dish and can also stand alone as a fuel powerhouse. Carry small packets of nuts or trail mix for an energy boost. Additionally, Justin's Naturally Delicious makes small packets of nut butters that are lightweight and a great source of protein. I like to add a packet to my oatmeal in the morning.

10 **Start your day right.** Trail coffee can be lackluster but not when it's instant coffee from Alpine Start. Their coffees use coconut milk and come in glorious blends such as Dirty Girl Chai and Coconut Creamer Latte.

HYGIENE PRO TIPS

1 **Get that clean feeling.** When I first heard about pee cloths, I wasn't interested. It seemed unappealing to carry a cloth clipped to the outside of my pack for the purpose of wiping after peeing. But now that I finally gave it a try, I won't get on trail without one. Having a pee cloth helps your clothes stay fresh longer and makes everything feel a bit more hygienic. As a hiking companion said after I gifted her one, "Well, that just made things a whole lot more civilized!"

2 **Manage the monthlies.** Women often wonder how to handle their period on trail. If you choose to use tampons, remember you'll have to carry out all your used feminine products. Personally, I use the Diva Cup with single-use antibacterial wipes to clean my hands before and after emptying it. With the Diva Cup, having your period while hiking is not a big deal.

3 **Chafe no more.** I have good-sized hips, and for some reason, they're shaped in such a way that backpacks can rub my skin off in painful lines. So before multiday trips with a heavy backpack, I cut long strips of moleskin tape and place them strategically along my waist. Their anti-chafing magic has helped keep my skin intact.

4 **Rethink your soap.** Clean hands at the end of the day are a delight, but liquid soap is messy and heavy. Enter Sea to Summit Pocket Soap Wafers. These dry soap sheets (they look a bit like Listerine breath strips) are biodegradable, easy to use, extremely lightweight, and will never leak in your bag.

5 **Everybody poops.** Pooping in the woods can be really intimidating if you've never done it. But once you cross that line, you'll join those of us who know just how glorious and liberating outdoor bathroom time can be. To make the experience easier and more hygienic, pack some Combat Wipes, biodegradable hygiene wipes that can be buried in your waste hole, the six-inch hole you dig before pooping (remember to bring a lightweight trowel to dig with; I recommend The Deuce Backcountry Potty Trowel by TheTentLab). It's important to feel clean and be environmentally conscious every time you use the bathroom outdoors.

6 **Luxuriate.** Small luxuries can make all the difference in the woods. For me, at the end of the day, a small spritz of deodorant is bliss. I fill a two-ounce plastic bottle with Crystal Essence's Mineral Essence Deodorant Spray. It's the perfect pick-me-up after a smelly day on trail.

7 **Mind your unmentionables.** Let's talk underwear. Cotton is not your friend on trail since it takes forever to dry, retains smells, and does not move well. Instead, wear underwear that has wicking properties and is odor resistant. In fact, a good pair of hiking underwear plus a pee cloth will help you feel fresh on trail for multiple days. ExOfficio is my go-to underwear brand.

8 **Try a backcountry bidet.** I have never personally used a backcountry bidet, but a friend of mine swears by it. It's a small attachment for a squeeze bottle (Smartwater bottles work well) to clean your backside. Using one of these reduces reliance on toilet paper and is 100 percent environmentally friendly (especially considering that you are reusing a plastic bottle!).

9 **Clean those teeth.** I'm a huge fan of clean teeth—in fact, my day doesn't really begin until I have a date with dental floss. But flossing on trail can be unpleasant if your hands and nails are encrusted with dirt. That's why I love Happy Eco's Plant-Based Floss Picks. You can floss while keeping those dirty fingernails out of your mouth.

10 **Don't forget the duct tape of the woods.** I like keeping a bandana attached to the outside of my pack as a multipurpose tool. It can be used as a napkin, a washcloth, a drying cloth, and so on—so many things! You'll be amazed at what one small piece of fabric can do.

Deciding what to pack is highly personal, though you should always include a good blend of lightweight gear and a few comfort items (hiking pillow? Yes please!). The following guide is a good place to start, but what ends up in your pack will evolve as you grow as a hiker. It's helpful to think of what you carry as different "systems." Identifying each system lets you create smaller sublists and helps visualize how everything will be used on trail and in camp. The primary list includes the items to bring as a backpacker; it is followed by items you will want to pack if you are staying in a hut system. This should be a good starting point as you plan a comfortable and safe experience in the backcountry. Enjoy your time!

CLOTHING TO WEAR ON TRAIL

Hiking pants or shorts
Hiking underwear
Hiking bra
Synthetic T-shirt
Midlayer long-sleeved shirt
Hat and/or Buff headband
Sun gloves (if there will be significant sun exposure)
Sunglasses
Trekking poles

CLOTHING TO PACK

Rain gear (I love the Outdoor Research brand)
Warm hat
Gloves
Sleepwear (lighter is better) or thermal bottom and top
Fleece jacket (if it will be cold outside)
"Sacred socks" (comfy socks that never leave your tent)

PACK AND ACCESSORIES

Backpacking pack (I love the brands Hyperlite Mountain Gear and ULA Equipment)
Waterproofing for pack (if your pack isn't made of waterproof material)
Stuff sacks to organize your items
Small bag for "day of" food (to be kept on the top of your pack)
Bear hang (or bear canister or Ursack bear bag if required or if there is heavy bear activity)
Waterproof phone case

SLEEPING SYSTEM

Sleeping bag or sleeping quilt
Sleeping pad
Pillow
Earplugs
Sleeping liner (if it will be particularly cold outside)

FOOTWEAR

Socks and liners
Gaiters (Dirty Girls are the best!)
Trail runners or hiking boots
Camp footwear (something like Crocs)

HYDRATION

Water bottle or bladder (I use the HydraPak 2L)
Extra water container to haul water (if water sources are far from camp)
Water-purification method such as pills or a filter (I use the BeFree Filter by Katadyn)

KITCHEN

Pot

Bowl (or you could just use your pot to keep weight down)

Mug for hot beverages

Fuel and fuel stove (I love the MSR PocketRocket)

Utensil (sporks are super convenient)

Cleaning rag

Pan scraper

Ignition

Sitting pad (like the Therm-a-Rest Z Seat)

TOOLS

First-aid kit

Foot care (moleskin, medical tape)

Leatherman Micra

Small-gear repair kit (Gear Aid has great products)

Phone

Watch

Satellite communication (optional but recommended—I use the Garmin inReach Mini)

Headlamp

Backup battery (Anker's are powerful and lightweight)

SHELTER

Tent, bevy, or hammock

Rainfly cover to protect tent from water

Ground cloth

Poles for assembling tent

Stakes

Guylines (rope to secure tent in addition to stakes) for extra tent security

NAVIGATION

Phone with map

Physical map or route notes, if useful

Compass (and learn how to use it beforehand!)

HYGIENE

Toothbrush (bamboo ones are great)
Toothpaste
Dental picks
Hand sanitizer/wipes
Camping trowel (such as The Deuce by TheTentLab)
Biodegradable wipes (I recommend Combat Wipes)
Backup toilet paper
Soap wafers
Lip balm
Sunscreen
Anti-chafing cream
Tick Key
Body wipes (optional)
Insect repellant

GEAR FOR STAYING IN A MOUNTAIN HUT

Great earplugs and a comfortable eye mask (for sleeping when others are up or snoring)
Reusable food container for lunches and leftovers
Dr. Bronner's Pure-Castile Liquid Soap for bathing and washing dishes
Mini metal clips for hanging laundry
Comfy shoes to wear in huts (I love OOFOS flip-flops since they help with foot recovery)
Clean clothes to lounge and sleep in
Plug adaptor
Proof of travel health insurance (your policy card)
Quick-dry towel

GRATITUDES

It has taken a lot of love, encouragement, and support for this city girl from Chicago to become a hiker. I have such deep gratitude for all the people who have joined me on trail, shared a meal with me in a mountain hut, inspired me with their stories, cheered me on when I was struggling, and taught me what it means to be a lifelong learner in this vast, beautiful world.

Thank you to my sweet friend, Amy, who constantly inspires me to lead with love and bring my best and brightest self to everything I do.

Thank you to the greatest sister, Danielle, who might not understand why I seek these ambitious outdoor adventures but is always available with a supportive word, enthusiastic encouragement, and unconditional love.

Thank you to my dad, Stephen, who gifted me with his courageous spirit and consistently says "yes!" to joining me on crazy adventures throughout the world.

Thank you to my mom, Ruth, who showed me that travel can be infused with spiritual wonder.

Thank you to my dear friend Emily, who helped me discover the magic of the mountains in my own home state and whose friendship and encouragement sustain me on trail and in life.

Thank you to the most fantastic Kenan, who pushes me out of my comfort zone on trail and inspires me to hike farther, climb higher, and never doubt what I am capable of.

Thank you to the amazing Hilary, my Alphabet Travel companion, who always encourages me to seek what is most beautiful, most profound, and most delightful in life.

Thank you to the adventurous Sarah, who is willing to hike with me in fun places throughout the world and whose company is pure joy.

Thank you to my high school best friend, Bobbie, who was one of the first people to show me the magnificence of the mountains. It breaks my heart that your precious life was one of the many casualties of the pandemic. I miss you.

Thank you to the fierce Jackie, who was by my side on my first major trek up Kilimanjaro and perpetually reminds me to keep laughing, keep striving, keep loving, and keep dancing.

Thank you to the delightful Lydia, who always encourages me to slow down and enjoy the wonder of the journey—and who inspires me to be brave and sleep alone in the woods!

And thank you to my beloved Matt. You invited me on the biggest adventure of all by asking me to walk next to you through our journey of life. Your unwavering love is my anchor in the world. I miss you every time I leave for an adventure and am immensely grateful to return to your arms once I arrive home.

ACKNOWLEDGEMENTS

Outside of my hiking and traveling community, there are so many people to thank for this book's evolution from a preliminary idea to what you hold in your hands today. This work is a tribute to the love, encouragement, inspiration, skills, talent, and countless supportive talks of many extraordinary individuals.

First, such a heartfelt thanks to Mamie Amine. You enthusiastically jumped on board to make this book a reality, and your dedication and innovation are what brought us to the finish line. Thank you for believing that this book could inspire women the way you inspire me!

Thank you to Kris McCoy for your exquisite editing. You infused this work with beauty and poetic phrase, and it's so much better because of your talent.

And for the others who provided their editing expertise—Beth Beasley, Hilary Hodge, Laura Kermaidas, and Jane Cook—my deepest thanks to you!

Amy Froelich! Your art heart and talent produced such amazing graphics for this book. Thank you for capturing the book's essence with your wonderful designs.

A big thank you to Caroline Smith for your beautifully unique and whimsical artistry. Your maps delightfully elevate my stories.

Maggie Powell, you made this book beautiful! Thank you for your gorgeous help with layout and all things visual.

To the team at Mindbuck Media, thank you for helping me bring this book into the world so that others might adventure along with me.

A bighearted thank you to Gold Leaf Literary, who helped provide a compass for me during this process.

Thank you to all my fantastic friends who listened with unwavering enthusiasm to my ideas, my progress, and my vision for what this book could be. My heart is full of gratitude for you all (and that means YOU, Evlyn Jackson, Sabine Boots, Jodie Appel, Sara Kahn, Adam Smith, Brenda Myers-Powell, Trevor Wayne, Betsy Burnette, Nita Carroll, Greg McCoy, Meghan Cizek, David Graangard, Renn Mahr, Lauren Parnofiello, Anne Ream, Rob Motley, Hanna Woody, Gary Whited, Billy Zanski, James Taylor, Al Satorelli, Michelle Renae, Alexis Solheim, Melissa Burdeos, Marta Williams, Heather Dickens, Kerry Bolinder, Laura Kermaidas, Daria Mueller, Kathy Reager, Deb Hall, Hui-Ling Kerr, Brad Keil, Shawn Verbrugghe, Dylan Rice, Rob Motley, Kirsten Peterson, Jodie Lawton, Debra Kayes, Kara Cura, Heather Laine Talley, Anni Bruno, Kaethe

Morris-Hoffer, Robin Lenner, Sabra Jensen, Jessica Bitter, Sara Ream, Niki Kordus, Missy Burgin, and Tim Peck).

Many thanks to those who have joined me on trail and inspired me to relish the journey and believe in my strength. Your tenacity and downright amazingness continue to motivate me to persevere: Esther Townrow, Anna Pfaff, Eva Hartman, Adam Pittman, David and Alex Riddleberger, and Keith Hanson.

And a deep-hearted thanks to Adventure Alan for always reminding me to hike my own hike.

Special thanks to my family. Each of you has been beyond incredible. So much love to my sister, Danielle, my father, Steve, my mother, Ruth, and my husband, Matt (and his entire family for their fabulous support!). May we all continue to find adventures big and small, inside ourselves and out, in the vast, beautiful world.

ABOUT THE AUTHOR

Rachel Durchslag is an avid hiker who has spent the last five years trekking some of the world's most magnificent mountain ranges. When not traveling, Rachel works in the healing profession, providing a range of alternative therapies to help people recover from trauma and create more room for joy in their lives.

Prior to her healing work, Rachel was the founder of the Chicago Alliance Against Sexual Exploitation, a nonprofit where she served as executive director. In her role there, she was dedicated to ending sex trafficking and sexual assault in Chicago.

Rachel is delighted to call Asheville, North Carolina, her home. She shares her life with amazing friends, her wonderful husband, Matt, and their mischievous dog, Maggie.